Will close
Two weeks.

Until he saw something at the bottom of the document that made him do a double take.

"You've gotta be kidding me," he muttered, then sat back on the bench. He read it twice to be sure.

Adapted from the novel Paws and Claws *by Maya Monroe.*

Maya Monroe. Just the sight of her name awakened something deep and unsteady inside him. Was it the same Maya Monroe?

Of course it was. Maya loved romance and always dreamed of being a storyteller.

He took a long, steadying breath. How could it be that his high school sweetheart still had this effect on him? When he thought about the women he dated over the past fifteen years: models, actresses, some of the most accomplished and interesting women on the planet...

And yet, a flash of Maya's red hair, the memory of her lips—soft, sweet, unforgettable—reduced him to nothing. He was toast.

The next few months were supposed to be devoted to researching and writing his screenplay. A serious drama. Now, not only was he returning to town to help his father, who could be...challenging, but he was about to bring to life a story by the woman he'd never left behind.

What were the odds?

Dear Reader,

Welcome back to Sunset County, where the charm of Main Street is rivaled only by the warmth of the fresh-baked cinnamon buns at Maya Monroe's bakery.

The holidays come early in this story when Maya's debut romance novel is optioned for film, and the producers decide to film in Maya's small town. Twinkling lights, gently falling snow and even a "rein-dog" parade transform Main Street into a winter wonderland—despite it only being October. But the biggest surprise for Maya isn't the premature holiday cheer—it's discovering that the director of the film is none other than her high school boyfriend, Will Hastings, now a renowned filmmaker. Let's just say their reunion is anything but smooth.

What I loved most about writing this story was how Maya and Will's creative tug-of-war mirrors their own history, and how they navigate their past highs and lows while turning Maya's creative vision into the movie of her dreams. It's a story about the beauty of second chances and the magic of a perfect "take two."

I hope you'll be swept away by the charm of Sunset County, the humor and heart of its residents, and the undeniable chemistry between Maya and Will. Most of all, I hope their story reminds you that it's never too late for forgiveness and new beginnings.

I'd love to hear what you think, so feel free to reach out and share your thoughts!

xo,

Elle Douglas

AUTUMN NIGHTS, HOLIDAY LIGHTS

ELLE DOUGLAS

SPECIAL EDITION

If you purchased this book without a cover you should be aware that this book is stolen property. It was reported as "unsold and destroyed" to the publisher, and neither the author nor the publisher has received any payment for this "stripped book."

Recycling programs for this product may not exist in your area.

ISBN-13: 978-1-335-18010-0

Autumn Nights, Holiday Lights

Copyright © 2025 by Elle Douglas

All rights reserved. No part of this book may be used or reproduced in any manner whatsoever without written permission.

Without limiting the author's and publisher's exclusive rights, any unauthorized use of this publication to train generative artificial intelligence (AI) technologies is expressly prohibited.

This is a work of fiction. Names, characters, places and incidents are either the product of the author's imagination or are used fictitiously. Any resemblance to actual persons, living or dead, businesses, companies, events or locales is entirely coincidental.

For questions and comments about the quality of this book, please contact us at CustomerService@Harlequin.com.

TM and ® are trademarks of Harlequin Enterprises ULC.

 Harlequin Enterprises ULC
22 Adelaide St. West, 41st Floor
Toronto, Ontario M5H 4E3, Canada
www.Harlequin.com

Printed in Lithuania

To my RTA pals—this one's for you.
Writing this story was like rolling the credits on the
many unforgettable moments and on-set adventures
during our undergrad years. Thanks for making
our university days pure movie magic!

Elle Douglas is a lover of '90s alternative music, a wannabe chef specializing in comfort food and a sometimes reluctant but usually dedicated gym-goer who lives in Toronto with her wife and their cat, Lucy (or Lucifer, depending on the day). Between writing romance novels and working as a high school guidance counselor, Elle works exclusively in helping others find their happily-ever-afters. Visit her at elledouglas.com.

Books by Elle Douglas

Harlequin Special Edition

The Vet's Shelter Surprise

Sugar Maple Farms

Her Fairy-Tale Farmer
Autumn Nights, Holiday Lights

Visit the Author Profile page at Harlequin.com.

Chapter One

August

The thing about macarons—those light-as-air pieces of pillowy pastel perfection that looked so cute and inviting tucked in colorful rows in the bakery's display case—was that they were finicky. Temperamental. Unpredictable.

Everything from the humidity in the air to the freshness of the eggs and the fine grind of the almond flour could make the difference between a perfect batch and one that was destined to be swept from the baking sheet into the trash, so any time Maya Monroe pulled a successful tray from the convection oven in her bakery, she couldn't help but feel like an alchemist.

And today, Lady Luck was on her side.

"Praise Pillsbury," Maya murmured, satisfied at the smooth surfaces of the twenty-four little desserts that she'd painstakingly piped the perfect distance apart only an hour earlier. Now, they just had to sit for forty minutes until they developed a nice skin that would prevent cracking, and then she'd place them in the display case at Flour Child Bakery for the residents of Sunset County to enjoy.

She set one of her many small digital timers, then

moved on to her next task, a batch of snickerdoodle cookies which were decidedly harder to screw up.

It was coming on five o'clock in the morning, almost two hours until opening time. As Maya labored in the back of her bakery, she let her mind wander to the plot of her current work in progress, a classic fake-relationship romance novel that was the second in a series she was working on. At this point, baking was second nature to her, and she could allow her mind to wander while she kneaded and shaped dough, sifted flour, measured sugar and piped icing.

Time to brainstorm during these moments of quiet and solitude was really the only perk to operating Flour Child on her own. If she could swing it, she would hire an assistant in a second, but although she had a steady stream of customers in the peak tourist times of her small cottage country town, she had to spread her revenues out over the course of the year, which included a slower winter season.

One of her timers dinged. Maya opened the other oven a crack and peered in at the pain au chocolat, perfect golden flaked tops shining in the light of the oven.

If only the main characters in her stories were as predictable as *most* of her recipes.

For the next two hours, Maya filled up her case with baked goods, placed paper-wrapped baguettes in the basket beside the cash register (she'd moved it there one day and was pleased to see how many people picked one up as an add-on to their orders; they were like the bakery version of the chewing gum and battery display at the grocery store) and cleaned and swept the back area.

Right before she flipped the sign at the door of the

bakery to Open, she took a moment in front of the mirror in the bathroom to apply a swipe of lipstick. She let her long wavy red hair free from her hairnet and straightened her apron over her sunflower-print dress.

There were already three customers out front when she unlocked the door, so when her phone rang from the counter behind the till, she ignored it.

"Morning," she said, grinning at the first person in line, an elderly man wearing a faded blue Sunset County Sailing Club ball cap, shopping bag clutched in his hand. "What can I get for you?"

"My wife sent me for a loaf of sourdough," he said, scanning the display case. "So I'll take one, sliced regular, and I'll take a couple of those lemon tarts, too."

"One sourdough and two lemon tarts," Maya said. "Anything else?"

"That's it."

Next in line was Noah Crawford, co-owner of the Briarwood Inn on Shaughnessy Lake. Up until recently, his wife, Grace, had done all of the baking for the continental breakfast they offered their guests. But they'd had a baby, and it was easier for Noah to drive the five minutes into town and pick up an assorted pastry order than for Grace to juggle an infant and an early morning in the kitchen.

"Here you go," Maya said, passing Noah the box of treats. "I tried a new recipe for cheddar and jalapeño scones. I threw some in, free of charge. Let me know what you think."

"Appreciate it," said Noah.

Maya smiled to herself as she turned to grab the box from behind the counter. Noah had the tired eyes of a new father who'd likely not slept a full night in a good long while.

The third customer was Cassie Foreman, a new regular who'd recently moved to town with her teenage son. Cassie's job as a web developer allowed her to work remotely. She'd once confided in Maya that the reason for her move had to do with the trouble her son was getting up to in the city, where he'd fallen in with the wrong crowd.

"How're things?" said Maya.

Cassie shook her head. "Honestly, no one prepares you for parenting a teenager. I used to think I was lucky to have a boy. Like I'd skip the raging hormones and everything. And I thought a change of scenery and a new school would be good for Lucas. But last week I got a call from his principal requesting a meeting on Monday morning. I haven't slept since. So now I'm here to eat my feelings. Any recommendations?"

Maya smiled sympathetically. "The blueberry muffins have been known to be a great distraction. Or you can't go wrong with the eclair."

"One of each please," said Cassie. "I mean, I hated high school. Who doesn't? But I kept my head down and did what I was told. It's like Lucas is intent on sabotaging his future. And my sanity!"

Maya felt for Cassie. And for Lucas, for that matter. Her high school experience had been a great one. She'd been a decent student, student council secretary and the lead in the musicals. She'd had lots of friends and was always on the invite to parties on the weekends.

That, and she'd spent most of her high school career head over heels in love with her boyfriend, Will Hastings.

Dates at the ice cream truck down at the docks. Cruising around the Sunset County lakes in Will's dad's old speedboat or in Will's pickup truck. Late nights lying in the hammock in her backyard, making out under the stars after her parents had gone to bed.

It was a perfectly idyllic time in her life, right up until Will abruptly ended the relationship.

He'd gotten a scholarship to Chapman University in California and all but left her in his sparkly Hollywood dust. Now, as Sunset County's most famous former resident, it was hard to forget he ever existed.

Where did Will Hastings live? visitors to the area would ask when stopping in at the bakery. The library kept all of his movie posters on display in their media section, and the local theater made a big deal every time one of his films was released, as though he was about to show up in town to walk the red carpets with his costars. Maya made a point to avoid anywhere in the vicinity of the Main Street theater on those nights.

But aside from the unhappy ending, high school had been a dream for her. It was too bad Lucas wasn't having the same experience.

"He'll come around," said Maya. Although Cassie was right to be concerned, from what Maya had heard around town about Lucas—a class-skipping, fake-ID-toting, back-talking kid with model-esque looks that landed him his choice of girlfriends, of which, apparently there were many.

"Why don't you stop by on Monday after your meeting with the principal?" Maya said.

"Better yet, maybe I'll come before and bring the poor woman something as a peace offering." Cassie rolled her eyes and held up her pastry bag. "In the meantime, I'll be enjoying these. Thanks, Maya!"

The bells above the shop door jingled as Cassie let herself out, and Maya picked up her phone from the counter to see who'd just called.

Valerie Easton's name popped up on screen. Valerie was Maya's literary agent, whom Maya had only signed with several months earlier after the moderate success of her first independently published series. Valerie lived in London, so her calls often came through early in the morning, since she knew Maya would be up.

Maya dialed her number, and Valerie answered on the first ring. "Hello, darling," Valerie's singsong voice sounded. "How are you getting on this morning?"

"Can't complain," Maya said. "I'm almost finished with the edits you suggested. It's taken a little longer than—"

"That's not why I'm calling," said Valerie, and Maya detected a hint of excitement in Valerie's voice beyond her usual cheery nature.

Maya took in a sharp breath and reached out to grab the wooden counter. Could it be? No. *No way.* In the split second before Valerie started speaking again, Maya's mind flashed through all the many inane reasons why her agent might be calling. A new headshot was needed. A podcaster had reached out for an interview. Some kind of tax form for international filing purposes was in her inbox and Valerie needed her to sign it.

There was no way, no how that Valerie was about to deliver any news related to the dream that Maya had done her best to keep at bay, since their conversation a month earlier about a project of Maya's that Valerie was shopping around to film producers.

"We've sold *Love on the Slopes*!" Valerie declared, just as the shop door opened again. Edith Campbell let herself in, trailing her shopping cart behind her. "Your book is going to be made into a movie!"

Maya gasped, Valerie's words cascading over her like a shower of glittering confetti. This had to be a dream—too dazzling, too surreal. Any second now, she expected flamenco dancers to spring up from hidden platforms beneath the bakery floor, a glowing runway materializing to lead her toward some imaginary stage. What kind of award did authors get for having their books turned into movies anyway? Whatever it was, she felt like she was already clutching it in her hands, ready to hoist it over her head.

She could have wept. This news was especially welcome given what she'd been dealing with over the past three months. Minnie, her beloved miniature schnauzer, had died after eight years of being her number one. The ache her absence had left behind had dimmed the light in Maya's life considerably.

"I—I can't believe it," Maya stammered, her voice barely above a whisper.

"I haven't even gotten to the best part," Valerie said.

Could there be a better part? How many holiday movies had Maya watched over the years, yearning to see her name in the credits? Her characters brought to life on the screen? And, to be honest, the extra paycheck for work that she'd already completed?

Luckily, Edith appeared to be taking her time surveying the bakery case. Maya turned her back slightly and waited for the best part.

"They want to shoot the film in Sunset County," Valerie exclaimed. "It's an American company, but they mostly shoot in Canada for the tax credits. And when they found out where you're from, they thought it would make great interstitial content to film the movie there and then have you interviewed as part of the promotion for it."

Maya almost dropped her phone. Her mind whirled with the possibilities. She was already picking out her outfit for the interview. That cute baby blue sundress with the scalloped sleeves? No. It had to be Christmas-y. Maybe the black-and-red gingham sweater with the gold buttons? Could she inquire about being an extra in one of her favorite scenes? Was this *really happening*?

"One thing, though," Valerie said. "If you sign, I just want you to remember, film is a very different medium than a novel. The company will be free to make any changes and adaptations they want. I'm just telling you that so you don't get disappointed if it doesn't go exactly according to your original story."

Before she could respond, Edith cleared her throat, and Maya remembered she had a customer.

"I'll have to call you back, Valerie," she said. She blinked at Edith, one of her most reliable customers who came every two days to buy either a loaf of pretzel or rye bread to share between her and her best friend, Margaret Anderson. Suddenly Maya remembered that not only was she a romance novelist who was about to have her book made into a movie, thank you very much, but she was also a proprietor of a business. One that, to be honest, paid the majority of her bills. *For now*, she thought.

Maya straightened her shoulders and placed her phone on the counter. "Hi, Mrs. Campbell," she managed to say. "What can I get you today?"

If Edith was picking up on the fact that Maya's heart was beating a mile a minute and that she was so happy that she might leap through the ceiling, she didn't let on. "I'll take a loaf of rye. And four sesame dinner rolls. And those macarons look delicious," Edith said. "My granddaughter and her friend are coming over after school. They're always taking pictures of their food." She waved her hand dismissively. "I think they'll like these. I'll take one in each color."

Maya grinned as she boxed up the treats and popped in four of her most Instagram-able cupcakes on the house for good measure because she was feeling celebratory. She rang up Edith's purchase, her mind still racing with the news.

"I hope the girls enjoy these," she said, passing the baker's box across the counter. "If they like them, tell them to feel free to tag me on social media."

Edith peered into the box. "You're a real sweetheart! The girls will love them."

"Have a nice day, Mrs. Campbell!" Maya practically sang.

She watched as Edith rolled her cart out of the bakery, clutching the treats that had turned out oh-so-perfectly: a true harbinger of the news of Maya's dreams.

Will Hastings exited the air-conditioned cabin of the Hy-Line Cruises ferry to the humid but breezy island air. As he waited for the passengers in front of him to shuffle down the platform, he surveyed the crowd departing the boat and the long lineup of those ready to take it back to the Hyannis seaport, glowing with suntans, kitschy souvenirs, their wallets a lot lighter than before they'd arrived on the island.

It was Will's first time on Nantucket, and even though he was fortunate to be able to afford a room overnight during a prime summer weekend on this short research getaway, he'd balked at the prices for even the quaintest of hotels.

The sun was beaming bright overhead, the air filled with the briny scent of sea air and fried clams from the restaurants on Wharf Street. A jazz trio heralded their arrival with a rendition of "Summer of '69."

Will plucked his small carry-on from the luggage cart, stood off to the side away from the other travelers and pulled up the directions to the Jared Coffin House, a bed-and-breakfast a short walk away. Phone in hand, he pulled his roller suitcase over the cobblestone streets, taking in the buzzing downtown, a mix of locals and summer people and the tourists who were just coming to enjoy the island for the day, with its collection of sandy beaches, gourmet restaurants and high-end shopping interspersed between the few tourist traps.

But Will wasn't there for a day of soaking in the summer atmosphere. After checking into his room and changing into a fresh T-shirt, he grabbed his notebook and a pen, pulled on a ball cap and made his way over to the Nantucket Whaling Museum on Broad Street. He had an hour or so to tour around the space before his meeting with Mitchell Stevenson, a local historian and whaling expert. Will was going to interview him for the script he was working on, a biopic on the life of Herman Melville, famed author of *Moby Dick*.

It wasn't necessarily a splashy box office heavyweight like many of the films he'd recently been hired for—but lately, he'd been harkening back to the time when the films he made were a little more artistic. Smaller in scale but deeper in meaning. Less CG, more well-crafted dialogue. A deeper message. Resonance.

"Here's your sticker," the friendly teenage girl at the front desk said. "You can come and go as you please. Gift shop's open until four o'clock."

"Thanks," said Will. He grabbed a pamphlet and gave the girl a quick smile, then rounded the corner to the gallery area of the museum. Guests were snapping photos of the giant whale skeleton presiding over the space, which included several artifact and interactive computer displays.

Just as he was approaching the replication whaling ship under the skeleton to read the placards, another volunteer approached the microphone. "We're about to begin the eleven o'clock screening," the man said. "Please take your seats."

Will had already seen the short documentary—Mitchell Stevenson had sent it to him in advance with a package of research materials—but he slid into a seat in the back row anyway.

As with so many of the topics that Will had researched over the years for his films, he was now fully consumed by the history of the whaling industry in the country, and the unbelievably harsh conditions the whalers had to face at sea. He watched the actors harpoon a CG whale and hold on for dear life as the giant creature flew through the ocean with them in tow. Will resolved to do his best not to be as crotchety when conditions on his film sets were less than favorable.

Will's phone buzzed in his pocket, and he slid it out to see his agent's name on the screen. He hit Ignore. The best part was just about to come on.

Just as he was about to slide the phone back in his pocket, the phone buzzed again.

Will slipped out of his seat just as they were about to get into the harrowing process of killing whales, and entered the brightly lit gift shop. Several shoppers were surveying the museum's offerings of books, scrimshaw replicas, tea towels and ship models.

"Richard," he said, tucking himself into the section of Christmas ornaments.

"Enjoying that fresh-caught lobster?" Richard said, no doubt about to tuck into a late take-out lunch in his small Brooklyn office.

"Not yet," Will said. "Everything's looking good for me to have a script for you to shop around to studios by Christmas, though. What's up?"

"That whaling project, Hastings? Might be a tough sell. But word on the street is Jacksonville Films is going full steam on the adaptation of the *Infinite Realm* series. I'm keeping my ear to the ground for you."

"Huh," said Will. He'd read the books—a hugely successful space fantasy series rivaled only by the likes of *Lord of the Rings* and *Game of Thrones*. One of the biggest budget franchises to come around in years. A couple of years ago, he'd have been salivating to take on a project of that scope. The thought of it now was…uncertainty.

"Anyway, in the meantime I've found you a project. Unbelievably, with all the specs you sent me."

Will bristled. Part of him was counting on Richard to dismiss his laundry list of demands as too challenging to deliver on so Will would have an excuse to avoid Sunset County that fall.

The other part of him, however, knew he was getting on a plane to Toronto and driving two hours north no matter what his job prospects were. Family, for better or for worse, would do that to you.

"I'm listening," Will said.

"Midlevel prod-co, but they've put out some solid stuff in the last few years. Good reputation for management and delivering on time. It's a quick shoot—three weeks max—so you can be in and out in the time you need to move your dad."

"Three weeks?" Will said. "What kind of movie shoots in three weeks?" Of the four films that Will had directed over the past six years, filming had taken place over the course of months, rather than weeks. The content required for a feature-length film, the locations and sets involved... The shoots always felt like a mini lifetime. He had friends in the commercial business who shot over days, but an entire movie in three weeks?

Not the kind of movies he was now used to dealing in.

"Well, about that..." Richard said. "Listen, before I tell you the details, I have to say, they're packaging it as a kind of...'Barbenheimer' situation."

"Like it's going to be aired next to a fluffy Barbie film?"

Richard cleared his throat on the other end. "You didn't like the Barbie movie?"

He liked Barbie fine. In fact, he'd had drinks a week earlier with Greta Gerwig, whom he admired very much. "Just give me the scoop," he said. He noticed the teenage girl at the front desk giving him a look, like she knew very well he was loitering to take advantage of the air-conditioning. He gave her a quick wave, then pretended to leaf through a book about Nantucket's indigenous Wampanoag roots.

"It's a Christmas movie," Richard spat out, as though if he said it quickly enough, Will would forget and move on to the other details. "They think it'll get great press if a director like you is involved."

Will groaned. The only great Christmas movie, in his mind, was *The Dead*, John Huston's adaptation of the short story by James Joyce.

"I know what you're thinking," Richard continued. "But listen. It's filming right on Main Street in Sunset County. A week of prep, a few weeks shooting, two or three contingency days. It's an even better situation than you were looking for. You said you wanted to be back in Brooklyn as quickly as possible, remember?"

Will paused. He'd initially asked Richard to find him a project anywhere near the vicinity of Sunset County, his hometown and where his father still lived. But Main Street? That was a five-minute drive from his Dad's house, and would make his trip to Sunset County that much easier. He had business to take care of, but he needed something to keep him busy while he was there if he were to maintain his sanity.

Maybe a fluffy movie like this, one that he could direct in his sleep while he took care of everything with his dad, was just what he needed. His business in Sunset

County could be wrapped up in a few weeks, if everything went according to plan. "Tell me more," Will said.

He listened as Richard gave him a more detailed rundown of the project.

"Send me the synopsis," Will said.

"Hold on," Richard said. "I'm sending it right now."

Will let himself out of the air-conditioned gift shop into the humid summer air and found a bench in the shade. He switched the call to speakerphone and opened the attachment from Richard's email.

"Love on the Slopes?" Will said incredulously and started to scroll. He scanned over the treatment, which confirmed everything he knew. He was a terrible choice for this project. "Set in the quaint town of Garrison Creek. A high-end wedding planner from the city named Sarah comes to the charming town to plan a wedding at the town's ski lodge, owned by her cynical ex-boyfriend Ben, who has a strict no-wedding policy…" He continued scanning the document. "Wait. What's a…*rein-dog parade*?"

Richard cleared his throat. "There's a parade of dogs dressed as reindeer. It's a Garrison Creek tradition."

Will couldn't help but scoff and noted the amused looks on the faces of a young couple who passed by hand-in-hand holding ice cream cones. Not only did it sound ridiculous, but wrangling a bunch of dogs on set sounded like his version of hell. "I don't know about this," he said. "And you're telling me there's nothing else shooting in the area in the next few months?"

"Other than this, it's dry," Richard said.

Will closed his eyes and took a deep breath. Three weeks. He could do three weeks.

Until he saw something at the bottom of the document that made him do a double take. "You've gotta be kidding me," he muttered, then sat back on the bench. He read it twice to be sure.

Adapted from the novel Love on the Slopes *by Maya Monroe.*

Maya Monroe. Just the sight of her name awakened something deep and unsteady inside him. Was it the same Maya Monroe?

Of course it was. Maya loved romance and always dreamed of being a storyteller, whether it was through her involvement in the school's drama department or the litany of short stories she was always tucking into his backpack, then demanding feedback on, as though he had anything to say about the cheesy romances.

He took a long, steadying breath. How could it be that his high school sweetheart still had this effect on him? He thought about the women he'd dated over the past fifteen years: models, actresses, some of the most accomplished and interesting women on the planet.

And yet, a flash of Maya's fiery red hair, the memory of her lips—soft, sweet, unforgettable—or the spark in her eyes when he'd so much as suggested a tweak in her performance as the director of the musical in their senior year, reduced him to nothing. He was toast.

The next few months were supposed to be devoted to researching and writing his screenplay. A serious drama, based on the life of one of the country's most enigmatic writers, who only gained acclaim for his now-famous novel after his death. Now, not only was he returning to town to help his father, who could be…challenging, but he was about to bring to life a story by the woman he'd never left behind.

What were the odds?

He pinched his nose, the weight of what he was heading into settling on his shoulders. Three weeks? It was going to be an eternity.

Chapter Two

October

Maya poured a splash of cream from a silver container into her take-out coffee cup, then fitted the plastic lid on top. She normally didn't drink coffee this late in the day, but she'd just hit a wall while closing Flour Child and needed some energy for her second job that day. A small coffee felt like just the kick she needed to get some words in over the next few hours before bed.

"Hey, Maya," a familiar voice called behind her.

She turned to see Andie Carter, one of her most loyal customers, standing in line with her boyfriend, Knox Walker. Andie owned and operated a children's birthday party center just down the street called Magical Beans and ordered all her cakes from Maya.

"Oh, hey!" said Maya. "I can't wait to show you my concept for the magic mirror cake for next weekend."

Andie looked up at Knox and grinned. "We have a Snow White party next." She turned back to Maya. "If it's anything like the magic carpet cake, I think you're going to break the internet again. I had a family from Sweden reach out last week to see if I did any traveling party coordinating."

"It'd be worth their while to bring you out," said Knox. "You're the best in the business."

Andie rolled her eyes and swatted at him, but clearly, she was lapping up the compliment. Knox and Andie had been friends since childhood but had only gotten together just over a year ago. Their wedding was scheduled for the new year, and they'd hired Maya to do their cake as well. Maya couldn't wait, not only to make the cake of their dreams, but to enjoy being a guest as well.

"I heard the crazy news about your movie," Andie said, eyes widening.

Her movie. It had been months since Maya had gotten the news, and the mention of it still gave her butterflies in her stomach. "I'm so excited," she said. "And it's filming in town!"

"Not only that, but the fact that it's gone super Hollywood," Knox said. "How'd they land Will Hastings?"

Maya blinked, and she felt her heart skip a beat in her chest. "I'm sorry?"

Andie and Knox looked at one another. "It was on the town's Instagram yesterday," she said. "You haven't seen?"

"Will Hastings. Directing a holiday romance!" Knox said. "I mean, you've gotta love it."

Love it? The sound of Will's name anywhere near her project made her feel like throwing up.

The excitement slowly drained from Andie's face. "Wait, didn't you…"

Maya steeled herself. She couldn't have a public meltdown, at least until she processed what Andie and Knox were saying. "We dated in high school, for like a minute," she said, waving her hand in the air and doing her best to smile, even though she wanted to punch a hole through the wall. She hadn't acted since high school and was surprised by how the skill was coming back to her.

"You're not involved with choosing the director or anything?" asked Andie.

Maya shook her head. "My only involvement was to cash the check for the rights to the story. The production company owns it now, and they can do anything they want with it." Which, apparently, included making her life hell on earth. "Sorry, I've got to run," she heard herself say. "I think I left something on in the bakery."

Pulse pounding, she exited Rise and Grind onto Main Street and furiously dialed Valerie's number.

"Maya," Valerie said. "Did you hear the great news? I just got off a flight from Hong Kong. I was about to call you!"

"Great news?" Maya hissed. "How is it possible that Will Hastings is directing my movie?"

"I thought you'd be thrilled," Valerie said. "Talk about star power! It's already causing a buzz on social media. Think of how many people who wouldn't normally watch this movie are going to seek it out. And that you're both from the same small town? Amazing!"

Maya's stomach churned. She thought about telling Valerie why the news was so catastrophic. Not only had Will dumped her unceremoniously and gone on to live a glitzy and glamorous life, the kind they'd dreamed about while lying in the hammock in her parents' backyard those summer nights so many years ago, but his success tracked with how they'd always been in high school. Will was always number one in everything: top student. Valedictorian. First choice for any leadership committee. She'd always felt a little like…not a hanger-on, necessarily. But she got used to existing in Will's shadow.

And now, Will had achieved his dream of making it big in Hollywood. And this—this was supposed to be her thing.

Will was about to ride into town on his high horse and have full control over a part of her that mattered so much. And not only that, she knew full well from reading interviews and listening to him on podcasts that Will had no respect for the type of stories she told. He found them trite. Formulaic. A complete eye roll.

"If you say so," Maya said weakly, her stomach sinking even further. "Bye, Valerie."

Coffee in hand, Maya stood on the sidewalk, gazing down at what would soon be the film set. It was supposed to be the most exciting week of her life, and now all she felt was dread.

The only saving grace was that from her stool at the counter of Flour Child, she'd have eyes on what was going on.

And there was no way, no how she was going to let Will Hastings and his pretentious, high-brow tastes ruin her party.

She walked up the familiar path to her bungalow just outside of town, digging through her purse for her keys, before unlocking the door and stepping into the quiet foyer. She'd bought the house from her parents five years earlier, when they decided to move closer to the city to be near Maya's brother, his wife and their two kids. Sunset County had been home for her parents all their lives, but the pull of their grandchildren was stronger than the comfort of small-town living.

Over the years, Maya had made the bungalow truly hers. The decision to paint the front door the color of cotton candy had raised more than a few eyebrows, but even Sam Lawson, the motorcycle repair guy three doors down, had to admit—grudgingly—that when the pink English climbing roses were in full bloom, the house looked like something out of a fairy tale.

She pushed open the front door and was greeted with the silence that she was still trying to get used to, even all these months later.

The loss of Minnie was always the most acute when she stepped into the entrance. The absence of the little friend who no matter what, treated her arrival home as if she were royalty. The wagging tail, the scrabble of excited paws on the floor, the gentle whine of pure joy at her return.

If she could buy that moment, just for one day, today would be the day.

Same old, same old, Will thought as he drove his rental car slowly down Sunset County's Main Street.

It was as though someone had hit Pause on Sunset County, and he'd just pressed Play by turning onto the main strip. The old guys sitting outside of the tackle shop trading barbs and tips on where the trout were hiding in the nearby rivers. The baskets of potted mums in rich marigold, ochre and burgundy hanging from the lampposts, compliments of the Sunset County Business Improvement Association. The lineup inside Pete's Pies, and the happy faces in the window downing a slice of their famous double-smoked cheese pizza. The neon glow of the Coors Lite sign in the window of the Hidden Oar Pub, where he'd duped the new bartender with his fake ID and celebrated his eighteenth birthday in spectacular fashion, or so the photos of the night told him the morning after.

Not much had changed, but for Will, seeing the small town that had been his whole world for the first eighteen years of his life now for the first time in over a decade, it felt unknown to him. Like one of his recurring bad dreams that involved stepping onto a film set and having no idea what movie he was supposed to be directing.

Upon closer inspection, there were a few new places he hadn't seen before: a women's clothing store called Wish. A couple of new bike racks and an empty storefront where his favorite comic bookstore used to be. And at the end of the strip of businesses, farthest from the water, with a sandwich board out front advertising pumpernickel bread and blueberry scones, a bakery called Flour Child.

Aside from the few new additions, Sunset County was like most small towns: frozen in time.

For the residents, a place worth preserving. And for the seasonal cottagers who spent their summers enjoying Shaughnessy, Hollyberry and Robescarres Lakes, a home away from home that promised the same reliable nostalgia as flipping through an old photo album, sepia-colored snapshots in time when all their favorite memories were made.

He came to a stop in front of the storefront office of Sunset County Realtors, then exited the car and felt the relief rushing to his legs after the long drive from Pearson Airport.

Will instinctively went to lock the door of the rental car, then paused. Did people still leave their cars unlocked around here? He tapped the button on the key fob and heard the click of the lock. He'd been gone for years, but surely some things had changed.

If he didn't have an appointment, he'd be tempted to take a walk down to the waterfront. It was the perfect fall day—crisp air, the autumn sun gleaming overhead and the leaves just a week shy of reaching their full spectrum of vibrant color.

But he had business to attend to.

A woman looked up from the front desk as he entered the office, and after a second, her face broke into a wide smile. "Well, hello!" she said, standing up and moving to the front to greet him. "You must be Will."

He extended his hand to shake hers. "Will Hastings," he said. "Nice to meet you."

"I'm Hayley Chapman. Come on in, have a seat."

Most realtors he'd worked with over the past several years donned designer suits and had professional hair and makeup. Hayley wore faded blue jeans and a knitted sweater, her hair pulled back in a ponytail. Maybe not the most professional, but according to an internet search, she and her business partner, Vibika, were the best in the area.

"Let me just pull up your email," she said, clicking on her laptop. "Ah, yes. The property out on Robin Point Road." She looked up. "Nice views there. It's been a while since something came on the market in that area... It'll sell quickly. When are you hoping to get it listed?"

Will cleared his throat. "The timing is still under discussion." One of the many conversations with his father he was dreading.

"How much work do you think it'll take to show? Any small renos or anything? Or just some usual staging?"

"Renos, not likely, although I haven't seen the place for a while. My dad has always been good at keeping things in order. I'm sure it'll be the exact same as it was fifteen years ago." *Order. Control. Tradition.* The qualities that drove a wedge between him and his father during his teen years, conflict they'd never really recovered from.

Hayley nodded. "Well, we've got a month, a month and a half tops before the snow comes, and the market slows down. I'd suggest trying to get the listing up sometime in the next few weeks if you want options. I'll send over my photographer whenever you're ready."

Will cleared his throat. "I was thinking in the next few days," he said. "I'm only in town for a few weeks."

"The film shoot!" said Hayley, clasping her hands together. She leaned in. "People around here are really excited." She grinned. "Hollywood comes to Sunset County."

Will forced a quick grin. Hollywood? He wouldn't go that far. The stars were two wash-ups who'd hit their peak in the early 2000s. Ginger Estrada had her moment in 2002 as a teen star in a three-part series of slasher films set at an elite New England boarding school, and Blake O'Connor was semi-well-known for his role in a short-lived drama series about a former NFL quarterback turned detective for hire. Their faces were recognizable in that *I know I know you from somewhere, but I don't know where* kind of way, but their acting skills were utterly forgettable. How he was going to coax a half-decent performance out of them, however, was a problem for another day.

"I'll speak with my father tonight and give you a call tomorrow," Will said. "But let's assume we're moving forward quickly. You just let me know when you're sending out your associate. If I'm not going to be around, I'll give you the phone number for my dad's personal support worker. She'll let you in the house."

"Got it," said Hayley. She walked him to the office door.

"Nice to meet you," Will said, extending his hand. "You came highly recommended."

Hayley shook his hand, her smile growing. "Maybe next time you're here, you can sign my *Auto Toon* poster," she said. "I loved that movie!"

"It's everyone's favorite of mine," Will said. *Auto Toon* had been his second feature film, chronicling the life of Bruce McCall, the visionary cartoonist whose whimsical illustrations of cars, futuristic landscapes and nostalgic Americana made him an icon in the world of art and humor.

Will's former agent had practically laughed him out of the office when he'd pitched her the idea—who would want to watch a movie about a guy drawing cars?—but the blend of humor, heart and nostalgia resonated with people of all ages and put Will on the radar as a director to watch out for.

The process of making that film had also been a case of life mirroring art: Will spent time researching Parkinson's disease, which McCall suffered from in his later years and was ultimately the cause of his death only two years ago. Will started to notice some of the trademark signs of cognitive decline during his infrequent phone conversations with his father: his speech was getting a bit slower, and Will noticed that Gene was having trouble finishing sentences or forgetting words midconversation.

When Will suggested the idea of his father seeing the doctor, Gene had dismissed him and blamed it on a lingering cold he was still getting over.

It was only when a neighbor discovered Gene walking along the side of the county road forty minutes away from his house, and Gene admitted he couldn't remember how to get home, that his father had agreed to a medical appointment. A series of tests had confirmed an Alzheimer's diagnosis, and now, with his father facing a certain future of challenges ahead, Will had finally gotten him to agree to move to a local long-term care home called Pinecrest Haven.

"You let me know when you talk to your dad," Hayley said. "I'll start the process of prepping the listing."

"I'll give you a call in the next day or so," said Will. "Appreciate your help."

He stepped out onto the sunny street, taking a deep breath of the crisp air. Maybe he'd swing by the bakery and grab something to bring home for his father—a half-hearted peace offering, a sort of apology for the long absence and the fact that it took selling the house he'd grown up in to finally bring him back.

Gene was going to have a field day when he found out the details of the movie Will was directing. The only saving grace was that it was tied to Maya Monroe. Gene didn't have a soft spot for much—he was downright ornery most of the time—but he'd always liked Maya. He'd written off Will's breakup with her as just another dumb mistake on his son's part.

The bakery was on his list of locations to scout over the next week: the scene where the male lead, Ben, takes the female lead, Sarah, for gingerbread cookies after the Christmas tree decorating contest was filming there. The smell of fresh baked bread was beckoning enough.

Will let himself into the bakery and scanned the case holding a variety of sweet treats and savory options, like pizza puffs and cheddar and chive tarts.

When the couple in front of him paid and moved aside, Will had to blink, momentarily stunned.

The woman behind the till was none other than Maya Monroe, wearing a flower-printed apron, her hair piled on top of her head in a neat bun and an expression of surprise tinted with annoyance in her eyes.

What was Maya doing working at a bakery?

"Will," she said. Her pursed lips appeared to be laboring to form a tight grin, long lashes lining her suspicious green eyes.

"Maya?" he said, still processing. "I thought you were a...writer?"

He immediately regretted not reaching out to her before coming to town. He knew from his agent that Maya was still living in Sunset County—and that the production company was planning to involve her in some kind of promotion for the film. He should've done the professional thing and contacted her to catch up before he arrived. But something deep down had told him she wouldn't be thrilled about his involvement in the project. And the look on her face confirmed it.

"I *am* a writer, as you likely know by now," Maya said. "This is my day job."

"How long have you been working here?"

"I own the place," Maya said.

Will scanned the bakery, the painted floral murals on the wall, the bubblegum pink curtains and kitschy kitten and pony knickknacks on the shelves, where blueberry and strawberry jams and red pepper chutney were also on offer. Of course she owned the bakery. Everything about it screamed Maya: bright, bubbly, colorful and in-your-face sweet. He didn't even need to taste the crème brûlée tarts, which, admittedly, looked amazing.

"It's…really cool," he said. "When did you get into baking?"

"After my undergrad," Maya said. "Turns out the job market wasn't overly saturated with positions seeking someone with a degree in Victorian literature."

The tension was thick in the air. Will knew he had to say something, to acknowledge the elephant in the room, that they hadn't talked since he'd broken up with her—over text, a stupid and cowardly move by any measure, and the thought of it made him wince—and how he was taking the reins on her project.

"Listen," he said, "I know this is kind of weird. I—"

"Kind of?" Maya said, her green eyes flashing with frustration. "Honestly, Will, it *kind of* feels like you're back here to…make fun of me or something."

Before Will had a chance to respond, the bakery door opened, the bells above tingling as a man and a young boy entered with a little chocolate brown puppy.

It took a moment, but Maya's expression shifted from irritated to overjoyed. "Now who is this little bundle of heaven?" she cooed, flipping the countertop up and moving out into the main space.

Will watched as she crouched down and gathered the little puppy into her arms and began showering it with kisses. Now that she wasn't hidden by the counter, Will took in her stunning curves. Maya looked just as beautiful as she did in high school, and maybe even better.

"We just got him yesterday," the young boy said, reaching over and scratching the little puppy's head.

"I've been wanting to adopt a dog for a while now," Maya said. "Dr. Carter over at the Sunset County animal hospital gives me the heads-up whenever a dog is dropped off, which isn't very often. I've met a couple of sweeties, but they've been too big for my place, or they're not hypoallergenic." She placed the puppy down on the ground. It wagged its tail as it gazed up at her. "But you," she said, "look like the perfect size."

"If you're serious," said the man, "when we picked up Clark last week, the breeder said that they had a cancellation from someone who'd been planning to pick up one of the litter. Apparently they found out last minute they'd be moving across the country for work. So there's one little fella who might be heading to the shelter if they don't find him a home." He dug his wallet out and passed her a card. "You could give the breeder a call."

"Thanks," Maya replied, accepting the card. Will noticed a brief flicker of sadness in her eyes as she spoke. "I'm still getting over losing my Minnie a few months ago." She quickly squared her shoulders, her expression shifting as she took on the role of the professional business owner once more. "And what can I get you?"

Will watched as Maya plucked the man's order out of

the case—a dozen sesame dinner rolls and a small carrot loaf—cashed them out and then bid them farewell. "Come back and visit any time, Clark!" she called, waving with a wide grin on her face as the man and his son exited the shop.

"A dog, eh?" said Will. "Who's Minnie?"

Maya glanced over, seemingly surprised he'd stuck around. "My miniature schnauzer. I lost her recently. So I'm just trying to figure out when I'm ready..." She paused. "Gets lonely back here sometimes," said Maya. "I think it's time I get an assistant. I've been working six days a week since I opened. So between that and writing...it's a lot."

"You really do all this on your own?" said Will. It looked to him there were about fifteen different options of baked goods available in the display case, never mind all the different loaves of bread piled up behind the counter. "This must take all day to bake."

"I've figured out some good systems," she said. "And some of the doughs and spreads work for multiple products."

She was being friendly but aloof, and Will sensed she wasn't really up for a catch-up session. Time to make his exit, but in an ingratiating way.

"Can you recommend something I can bring home for my dad? I can't choose. Everything looks too good."

Maya didn't react to the compliment. "How is Gene?" she asked. "I used to see him now and then down at the docks fishing on weekends. But it feels like it's been a couple of years now."

"He's hanging in there," said Will. "But he's getting on." It didn't feel like the right time to burden Maya with his family drama. He needed to make his order and let her get on with her day.

"He liked lemon, didn't he?" she asked, folding a cardboard box together. She plucked out a lemon Danish and placed it in the box.

"Good memory," said Will. "I'll take a couple of those, thanks."

She added another pastry. "But you didn't like lemon. You," she said, plucking a cinnamon roll from the shelf below, "preferred cream cheese frosting."

Will had to smile. "Still do."

He reached for his wallet, and she waved him away. "On the house," she said. "Welcome back to town, Will."

Chapter Three

Maya exhaled as soon as Will disappeared through the doorway, box in hand, and leaned up against the counter for support.

She hadn't expected to see him until the film started to shoot, when she intended to be close by to observe what was going on and potentially intervene if she noticed Will taking her story in the wrong direction. Meaning anything that was a departure from her carefully constructed plot and thoughtful character development.

But what she hadn't prepared for was the sudden wave of warmth that hit her, like she was a hormonal teenager all over again. The magnetic pull she'd felt for Will all those years ago was still there, but now, it had taken on a new layer. The slight crease in the skin lining his deep brown eyes. The light stubble on his sculpted chin, and the way he'd grown his hair out a little from how he'd worn it in high school. He worked in the arts but could have been mistaken for a member of an Olympic rowing team. Athletic, strong, with an effortless grace that carried him wherever he went.

Not only was Will annoyingly successful, but he, somehow, had become even more impossibly attractive. Her plan for him to see her again for the first time at her best—not after a long day of baking and serving customers, but with her hair freshly blown out, makeup and that navy blue dress she knew full well showcased her figure better than anything else she owned—had gone up in a puff of powdered sugar.

Having him in her bakery, complimenting her business and her products... It was satisfying. She hated that she cared about impressing him, but the appreciation in his eyes at her teeny tiny bakery in his old small town... It wasn't nothing.

Her cheeks burned, and it suddenly felt like the temperature in the bakery had risen by ten degrees.

She came out from behind the counter and propped open the front door of the bakery. The early October day still carried a lingering trace of summer's warmth, and it never hurt to let the sweet scents from inside free to coax any passersby into making an impulse purchase.

She stole a glance down the street, just in time to see Will sliding into his car. The charming wunderkind of Sunset County was back, and for the next few weeks, she'd have to keep her composure around him. Not just for the sake of her pride, but to save her film.

Maya busied herself for the next two hours, moving things around on the racks, cleaning countertops and the glass of the display cases and making her delivery orders for the following week, but it was a challenge to keep their interaction from running through her mind on replay.

Just as she was about to flip her sign to Closed, Cassie Foreman appeared in the doorway, Lucas in tow and looking like the last thing he wanted to be doing was accompanying his mother to do errands.

"Sorry, I know you're trying to close up," said Cassie, her voice apologetic. "Any chance you have any baguettes left?"

Maya held the door for Cassie and Lucas. "We're out of baguettes, but I have one more sourdough Vienna loaf."

"Perfect," said Allison. She glanced sideways at her son, then gave Maya a *look*. The look of a mother who knew the importance of a delicate approach for what she was about to say. "We're just handing out résumés," she said in a singsongy voice. "Lucas is looking for a part-time job, as per the suggestion of his principal."

"Under duress," Lucas muttered, sliding his phone out of his pocket and absent-mindedly scrolling through some photos.

"What kind of job are you looking for?" said Maya. She slid a loaf of bread into a paper sleeve and tucked a couple of croissants in that would go stale overnight.

"The kind that keeps him out of trouble," said Allison. She gave Maya another look, the one of a mother who'd had it up to here. "But unfortunately, Lucas is learning that his reputation precedes him. We've had more than one raised eyebrow today at the idea of hiring him."

"Mom," said Lucas. He scoffed and stuffed his phone in his pocket. "Can we go? I have homework."

Allison laughed. "Ha!" she exclaimed. "You think I'm going to buy that?" She looked at Maya. "More like there's an NFL game on that he's tracking for his fantasy league."

Maya smiled, resisting the urge to laugh. "Why don't

you leave a couple copies of your résumé," she said, "and I'll pass it along to any local business owners who come through who might be looking for help."

"Thanks, Maya," said Allison. She looked at Lucas expectantly.

"Thanks," he muttered.

Maya followed them to the door, turned the sign over and locked the door before any other customers tried to squeeze their way in.

Will was in town. Her movie was about to start.

But there was no room for distractions. She had two chapters to finish tonight.

Like the rest of Sunset County, the Hastings home on Robin Point Road at the edge of Robescarres Lake appeared frozen in time.

The black-eyed Susans still swayed gently in the breeze, lining the front garden that stretched across the face of the single-story house. The same red shutters framed the windows, and Will's basketball hoop remained fastened above the garage. His dad's old truck was likely parked in the garage—for good now, Will realized. Despite Gene's health issues, the house was surprisingly tidy, well-maintained, as if the years hadn't worn it down at all.

Will left his suitcase in the trunk. Staying with Gene for the duration of the shoot was out of the question, especially given the hours he'd be keeping. Instead, he was staying with the rest of the crew at the Briarwood Inn, not too far away on Shaughnessy Lake, where his early morning wakeups to get to set on time and late nights making phone calls and script notes would be tolerated.

He got out of the car and took a moment to breathe in the scent of the forest. Earthy pine and dirt. It was grounding.

He knocked on the door, not to get his dad up but just to let him know he was coming in, and let himself into the front entry.

A woman in her late fifties with dark hair tied back in a bun and a warm smile that reached her eyes popped her head out from the kitchen. Her skin, rich and warm like dark honey, glowed against the soft lavender of her scrubs and the cardigan draped over her shoulders. "You must be Will," she said, smiling. "It's nice to finally meet you."

"Hey, Agatha," Will said. He'd spoken to his father's personal support worker a number of times on the phone. Had he known her presence was so warm and reassuring, he might have been a little less worried about the old guy than he had been for the past several months. He knew one thing, though: the fact that this woman had stuck around for more than a few days meant she was a saint.

"The prodigal son returns," a loud voice called from the living room.

Will raised an eyebrow and gave Agatha a quick grin. "Sounds like he's in good spirits," Will said.

"He's been looking forward to seeing you," Agatha said.

Yeah, right, thought Will as he kicked off his shoes, then hung his jacket on the hook near the door. The only thing Gene Hastings had ever looked forward to was a cold pint of Miller Lite on a Friday after work, his one indulgence of the week, and the latest issue of *National Geographic* arriving in the mail.

Otherwise, Gene had always lived a life of deferred gratification. Practicality. A good honest day's work. So it shouldn't have come as any surprise, all those years ago, when Will had announced at the dinner table that he'd been offered a full-ride scholarship to Chapman University in California to study film production, that Gene had put down his fork and looked at Will like he'd just announced he was joining a Tibetan monastery. "And what the hell do you think you're going to do with a degree in film production?" he'd asked.

Will had, for a brief moment when his acceptance letter came through, allowed himself to indulge in a daydream where Gene had patted him on the back and told him how proud he was of his son. Chapman was competitive, and Will had worked hard on the demo reel and portfolio, as well as the essays required for admissions.

But instead, he'd been met with the familiar mixture of scorn and skepticism that pretty much summed his father up.

"You're graduating top of your class. You've been given an offer to study engineering science at the University of Toronto," Gene said. "That's one of the most rigorous and respectable programs in the entire country. Explain to me why you'd give up that opportunity?"

"I didn't even want to apply there," said Will. "You made me."

His father's eyes steeled. "Not many people have the same academic gifts as you," Gene said. "You need to take that talent and put it to use in the world. Do something productive. Worthwhile. Something the world actually needs," he said, waving his hand in the air. "I'll tell you what we don't need. A single other nonsense movie."

Will remembered staring at the steamed carrots and pork chop on his plate. "It's a full ride, Dad," he'd said. "Do you know how much money that is?"

"And do *you* know how hard I've worked over the years, coming up with enough money to fund your education?" Gene said. "I'm not concerned about the money. I'm concerned about your future. You're going to U of T. Discussion over."

As it turned out, no parent signature was required for Will to accept his offer to Chapman. With the money he'd earned spraying down golf carts at the club outside of town over the past two summers, he'd booked a one-way flight to Los Angeles for that August and used the rest of his savings to outfit his small shared residence room with a comforter and sheets from the nearest Walmart and a *Donnie Darko* poster, which, in retrospect, was a pretty cliché and predictable choice.

But once he'd broken free from Sunset County and started his classes, he knew he'd made the right decision. But it also meant that it would be a long time before he could go home.

He was angry at his father, but he also couldn't shake the guilt. He knew, despite Gene's gruffness, how hard he worked to save that money for his tuition. It was a matter of pride, and so was the fact that Will had been accepted to an esteemed engineering school.

He pictured his father down at the sawmill, telling the other workers about his son's academic accolades, and his bright future ahead as a successful engineer.

Will got his mathematical mind from his father; Gene was brilliant. But his own dreams had been cut short when both his parents died when he was a teenager. Instead of pursuing an education, Gene had stepped in to care for his three younger siblings, taking a job at the local sawmill, where he'd spent the rest of his life.

The mix of Will's guilt and hurt, matched by Gene's stubbornness and disdain for Will's choice, meant their relationship, which had already been challenging, became ever more fraught, reduced to terse phone calls every few months, awkward excuses for missing holidays and eventually an unspoken acceptance that theirs would never be the kind of father-son bond you saw in movies.

This wasn't the kind of homecoming Will had pictured, but here he was.

Will entered the living room, with the bay windows overlooking the lake, to find Gene sitting in his easy chair, the twenty-four-hour news channel playing and a cup of orange juice beside him on a TV tray. "Hey, Dad," he said.

Gene looked more frail than he'd expected. The creases around his eyes and on his forehead had deepened since the last time he'd made a trip to New York, five years ago, at Will's insistence that he come for the screening of his first big film.

His skin had a new quality that was slightly more transparent. The only thing that hadn't really changed was his hairline: he still had a healthy thick crop of hair. It was ash gray and neatly trimmed, which Will suspected Agatha might have had a hand in maintaining. His shoulders were more stooped now, and when Will sat down across from him, he was struck by how his father's normally stern expression had softened into something else—was it hollowness? He was only seventy-four, but he might as well have been one hundred.

Gene's eyes locked onto Will's. Whatever was going on with him health-wise hadn't muted the strength of that familiar steely gaze. "What, you're not coming hand in hand with Julia Roberts? And here I was this morning, having Agatha pick out my nicest shirt."

At least his sass hadn't gone anywhere.

"She dumped me last week," Will said. "But I said I'd pass along your number."

Gene chuckled. "Good man."

Will placed the box of pastries on the table and opened the top. "Here," he said. "I picked these up in town. Did you know Maya Monroe has a bakery on Main Street?"

Gene paused for a moment. "Did I know that?" he said. "Maybe." He peered in the box. "Lemon Danish. My favorite."

"She remembered that, actually," Will said. He pulled a tissue from a box on the coffee table, placed the pastry on it and passed on to his father.

"At least someone's doing some remembering," Gene said. "It was the damnedest thing the other day. Your aunt Nancy called and asked me what I wanted for my birthday. I couldn't even for the life of me remember when it was."

"October twenty-seventh," Will said.

"That's what she told me." Gene shook his head and looked out the window. "It's like my head's emptied out."

Will allowed some space in case he had more to say, but he just stared out the window. He took a moment to look closely at his father. He'd planned on waiting until later to bring up the sale but sensed an opening.

"Listen, Dad," he said. "I was at the realtor's office

today. She was wondering when we might want to get the listing up. Have you thought about it at all?"

Gene tore his gaze away from the lake and looked back at Will. "I thought we could talk about it over dinner. Can you ask your mother what time it'll be ready?"

Will blinked, momentarily thrown by the question. He took a breath, keeping his tone gentle but firm. "Dad," he said softly, "Mom passed when I was three, remember?"

Forty-one years old. Cervical cancer. The only memories he had of her were in the thick photo albums neatly arranged on the shelf in the guest bedroom—albums that stopped abruptly after her death, as if the family had ceased to exist when she died.

Will watched his father, waiting for some flicker of recognition, some sign that the truth had pierced through. But Gene simply took another bite of his Danish, letting out a grunt of satisfaction. "Well then, I guess we're ordering in."

Chapter Four

By the time Maya finished locking up the bakery on Saturday afternoon, three white trucks had already rolled into Main Street. A group of crew members was unloading equipment into the vacant store at the foot of the street, right across from Rise and Grind. The back door of one truck was wide open, revealing an impressive array of gear—sturdy boxes stacked high, tripods and an endless tangle of cords and extension cables draped along the walls.

A woman with a clipboard was barking orders, overseeing the organized chaos. Maya couldn't help but shiver. It was really happening.

Soon, a section of Main Street would be transformed into a winter wonderland, ready for the first shoot day on Monday. Maya was planning to walk into town and snap a few photos of the set to send to her parents. They were coming up from the city later in the week to visit the set when Maya's short scene as an extra playing the town baker was shooting.

But that was tomorrow. For now, Maya had a date with her laptop and a grilled cheese. She double-checked that the bakery door was locked and set off down the sidewalk toward home.

The most wonderful thing about living in a small town was that it was, well, small. Maya's cozy bungalow tucked away on Edith Street was a quick ten-minute walk (or, if she was running late after too many taps on the snooze button, seven and a half at a hearty walk-jog) from downtown. She relished the walk to and from each day, even on dark February mornings when the air was so cold it froze the hairs in your nostrils when you breathed in. If she bundled up appropriately, ten minutes wasn't enough time to be uncomfortable, and after a fresh coating of snow, she loved how the road twinkled in the light of the streetlamps that lit her way.

Today, though, the elements were at their best. The early October conditions were perfect to walk home through: it was warm, with only a slight breeze in the air, just enough to run through her hair, let down after being pulled back all day. The early evening sunbeams broke through the trees and warmed her skin as she inhaled the grounding scent of freshly fallen leaves.

She only made it a few steps away from the bakery when the ringing of her phone from her purse cut the peace of the moment. She dug through and pulled it out to find an unfamiliar number on the screen. "Hello?" she said.

"Maya, this is Shauna Collins," a woman's voice sounded through the speaker. "I'm the production coordinator for *Love on the Slopes*. Your agent gave me your contact information."

"Oh hi, Shauna," Maya said. Her mind raced with what Shauna would possibly be calling about. Was her imposter syndrome not as unfounded as she'd thought, and the production company was pulling funding at the last minute? No. She'd just seen proof of filming with her own eyes. Was Maya being offered an actual part, not just the extra role she was scheduled for that Thursday? Was Shauna calling to share the good news that they'd replaced Will with another director?

"Not sure if you've seen any of the trucks on Main Street, but we've pulled into town, and we're excited to start filming tomorrow."

"I just saw," Maya said. "I can't wait to see everything all set up."

"You're going to love it," Shauna said. "Our set designer is amazing."

Her words gave Maya a thrill of delight.

"Listen," Shauna continued, "I know it's kind of short notice, but we've got a production meeting over lunch tomorrow at Ciboulette on Main Street. Just to go over final details for Monday. I understand you live close to town. Just wondering if you wanted to come by and say hello to the main cast and crew? I'm sure everyone would love to meet the woman who brought this story into the world."

"I'd love to," Maya said. "What time?"

"We're meeting at one o'clock. So I'll let the restaurant know to add one more seat?"

"Yes. I'll be there. Thank you."

"See you then," said Shauna. "Looking forward to meeting you."

Maya slid her phone back into her pocket, a rush of excitement bubbling up, but it was quickly overshadowed by something else. It should've been another perfect moment in this whirlwind journey, but the familiar wave of anxiety crept back in, relentless as ever. The idea of stepping into a room where Will was in charge had her nerves on high alert.

She pictured walking into the restaurant and the producer introducing her to the production team: the first and second assistant directors, the production coordinator, the director of photography and the production designer, all of the people charged with bringing her vision to life. It should've felt like a victory, but the knowledge that everyone in that room answered to Will, and the thought that they were probably wondering why he was even involved with her project, kept her mind racing.

And of course, she'd have to face him again. There was no way around that.

The idea of going home to an empty house was extra dangerous as she approached the top of Main Street, where the storefronts stopped and the strip of neighborhood homes began. As she did every day, Maya did her best to avoid looking at the charming brick structure that stood just to her left.

It was just another building. A place that happened to be on her walk home, a route she had no other choice than to take. Nothing to see here, folks.

And just like every day when she passed the gate opening to the path leading up to the door of the Sunset County Animal Shelter, she imagined the little barks and yaps and meows calling to her like a siren's song, and summoned every ounce of her will to keep walking right on by.

As always, the familiar lyrics from the Dionne Warwick song echoed in her mind: *I just can't get over losing you, and so if I seem broken and blue, walk on by, walk on by.*

She was broken, all right. And she was blue. She missed Minnie so much it ached, and it would take time to be ready to welcome another pet into her life.

Just as she was about to pass the gate, something inside her—something beyond her control—took over. And in that moment, there was no way, no universe, in which she could walk on by.

Maya entered the Sunset County Animal Shelter and found Freddie, the vet tech, at the front desk on his laptop. He looked up as she entered and grinned.

"Here to scan the pamphlet section again?" he asked, a knowing smile on his face.

Okay, so she'd given in to her impulses more than a few times over the past few months. But she'd only once made it past reception. Freddie was generally happy to engage in some friendly conversation, and she gathered she wasn't the only Sunset County resident on the fence about bringing a new friend into her life. Maya appreciated his lack of salesmanship, and he seemed to appreciate her hesitation—after all, the shelter didn't want to push anyone into adopting a pet only for it to end up returned after a few weeks.

Maya surveyed the ceiling of the shelter, as though she was a local building inspector brought in to assess the structural integrity of the space. *Looks like it's all up to code*, she imagined herself saying, clipboard in hand before making her way to the bathroom to test the plumbing.

Instead, she let her gaze connect with Freddie's. "I heard—" she swallowed. "I heard there might be a little schnoodle pup here." Her breath caught in her throat. Half of her hoped that Freddie would say *darn it*, only a couple of hours earlier someone had come and adopted the lucky little guy. But instead, Freddie's eyes lit up, and Maya knew that she was done.

"I hope you've cleared out the next few weeks from your calendar for puppy training," he said. "Because once you meet Bruce, there's no way you're going home without him."

Maya raised an eyebrow. "You know the deal, Freddie. It has to be love at first sight. Because this pup and I are going to be each other's one and only for a good long time, and it's important that we're a match."

Freddie grinned. "I know I was certain that you and the Australian shepherd were going to be soulmates—"

"But then you found out I'm allergic." During another weak moment, on a Sunday morning in September when she'd wandered in after waking up in the morning, reaching over for Minnie on the pillow beside her to find it empty, she'd roused herself from her only day to sleep in, thrown on her clothes and walked over to the shelter only to find that of course, the shelter didn't open until ten on Sundays.

It had felt like a sign from the universe Freddie was there, doing the chores early so he could make it to the city in time to take his mother to the theater for her birthday. He'd brought Maya back to the kennels and deposited the pup in her waiting arms. The little fellow had been so sweet, with ice blue eyes and the softest fur, but Maya was limited to hypoallergenic breeds that wouldn't have her sneezing all over the bakery counter and grossing out her customers.

"Follow me," said Freddie. He led her down the hall

to the last room on the right, past the bunnies, the amphibians and the cat kennels.

The wall was lined with cages, some empty and some with little pups looking out the gates. Maya could barely make eye contact: she would take them all home if she could.

"This," Freddie said, lifting a little reddish-brown ball of curly fur out of one kennel and depositing it into Maya's arms, "is Bruce."

The second the warm little pup, who felt like he barely weighed eight pounds, looked up at her with his deep black eyes, Maya almost wept. She cradled him close against her chest, then leaned down and breathed in his new puppy scent. He nuzzled her cheek, and she just about melted into a puddle on the floor.

"Can I bring him home today?" she heard herself saying.

"I'll draw up the paperwork," Freddie said, grinning. "I don't want to say it, but—"

"You can say it. You told me so," Maya said. Freddie left for the front desk. "And *I'm* telling *you* that I'm going to take very good care of you," she whispered to Bruce. "Although I'm not so sure about your name."

Bruce let out a little yap, and Maya laughed. "Okay, okay, I'll think about it," she said. "A pup by any other name would be as sweet, I suppose."

"The whole litter was named after superhero alter egos," Freddie said from far away. "Peter, Bruce, Clark, Diana, Tony."

"That's actually kind of funny," said Maya. "All right, I'll think about it."

Before leaving the room, she glanced around at the

other dogs, and the sadness she felt for them dissipated. The shelter was a warm and loving place. They were well cared for by Dr. Mel Carter and by Freddie. And one day, the right family would find them and bring them home, too.

An hour later, she was walking through her front door with Bruce in his kennel, a bag of food in her purse and her house feeling a little less empty than it had when she'd left that morning.

"Welcome to your new home," she whispered as she unlatched the door of the carrier. Staying crouched to the ground, she watched as Bruce emerged, with zero hesitation, and began to sniff around the corners of the rug, then galloped his little body into the kitchen to continue his exploration.

Suddenly her home was once again filled with love and companionship. How had she ever thought she needed more time before she could be whole again?

Chapter Five

"Looks like beautiful weather all next week," said Shauna, looking up from her phone. Will and his production coordinator stood at the host station at Ciboulette, another new place that had opened since he'd left town. For a Sunday afternoon in the off season, the restaurant was busy. Almost every table was full, and given the inviting aromas and delicious-looking dishes that passed by in a waiter's arms, he could see why.

It was a lovely place—far more polished than the diner that had once occupied the space. But with the influx of wealthier cottagers to Sunset County in recent years, it wasn't surprising that a few spots catering to a different crowd had sprung up.

Will shifted his focus to Shauna's phone, which she was holding out for him. The forecast showed a week of warm temperatures and sunshine, which wasn't always a given in the area. He could remember more than one October day in his youth when snow had unexpectedly blanketed Sunset County. "Think we should move the dates for the interior scenes?" Will asked.

Shauna adjusted her wire-rimmed glasses. "That's what I was thinking. We can swap the tree trimming for the Christmas tree farm visit and maybe switch the days for the bakery scene and the hot chocolate walk. The only thing we can't change is the rein-dog parade—I checked with the animal handler, and two of the four dogs she's bringing are already booked for a car commercial shoot next week."

Will had to fight the urge to shake his head at the sheer absurdity of the whole thing—a *rein-dog* parade, really? But Shauna didn't flinch, as if this was just another ordinary day in the world of holiday romance movie-making. He was already bracing himself for the many times he'd have to bite his tongue over the next few weeks if he wanted to keep things running smoothly. "Sounds great," he said, keeping his voice even.

A waiter approached the hostess stand. "Follow me," she said, "most of your party has already arrived."

Will followed the waiter and Shauna through the busy restaurant to the back room, which they'd reserved for lunch and the initial production meeting.

There were three seats left at the table, where the main crew members were assembled, as were the leads, Ginger Estrada and Blake O'Connor. The two actors were seated side by side, and Will was pleased to note that they looked great together and, as far as he could tell at first glance, were getting along. He'd been on his fair share of sets where the chemistry between the leads was a matter of movie magic, and between takes, the vehement dislike they had for one another was palpable.

"Everyone," Shauna said, drawing attention to the group gathered around the table, "I know some of you have already had Zoom calls with Will, but now that we're all here in person, please welcome Will Hastings, our director!"

The room filled with applause. A woman with short black hair and striking red lipstick stood up, extending a hand. "Welcome to the world of artificial snow and happily-ever-afters," she said with a playful grin. "I'm Caroline, the production designer." She shook his hand firmly. "I have to say, the set in the garden scene from *California Gold* was a huge inspiration for me."

"That was all Laura Wong," Will replied. "She's the visionary behind it."

The introductions continued. Cam, the director of photography, was a tall, wiry guy with a thick beard and tattoos that told stories of their own. Skylar, the first AD, was a bubbly woman in her late twenties, full of energy. Beside her sat Stu, the second AD, a man in his early sixties with an unimpressed expression—someone who had undoubtedly seen it all. He'd already met Brent, the producer, and Laura, the exec producer, a couple of times online, so after shaking hands with Ginger and Blake, Will settled into his seat.

"We can't wait to see what you do with this project," Ginger said with a smile that bordered on too wide. "I think I can speak for all of us when I say we're really excited to have you on board."

Were they, though? Will couldn't shake the feeling that before his arrival, there had been some quiet eye rolls, a shared skepticism at the thought of an outsider—someone who didn't belong to their tight-knit world—invading their space. A world with its own rhythms, its own ways of doing things. Would they really embrace him, or was this just a polite facade?

"Likewise," Will said, hoping he sounded convincing.

"I've got some ideas for the creative direction, and I'm looking forward to working with you all."

"Hopefully not *too* creative," came a voice from behind him, laced with both humor and something else.

He turned to find Maya standing in the entrance to the private room, wearing a fitted navy blue and white polka dot dress, her hair in loose waves around her shoulders. When he'd seen her in town it had been pulled back, and now he could tell it was just as pretty as it had been all those years ago. Her green eyes glinted with a mix of mischief and challenge, making his pulse flicker unexpectedly.

"Maya," said Brent. He stood up. "Everyone, I'm delighted to introduce you to Maya Monroe, the author of the book our film is based on. Maya lives in Sunset County, so we thought we'd invite her to join us for lunch. You'll probably see her around the set, too."

"And don't forget the bakery scene," Maya said. "I've been practicing."

Everyone around the table started to applaud again. Was it just him, or was it more enthusiastic for her?

Maya grinned widely and gave a quick curtsy. "Thank you for having me," she said. "I know this is a working lunch, so I'll just listen in. I'm so interested to know what happens behind the scenes."

Will watched as Maya's gaze swept over the table, landing on the only empty seat—directly next to him. His stomach tightened, but he forced himself to remain calm. He could do this. He could sit through lunch beside Maya and still keep his focus on the task at hand: getting his team ready for their first shoot day tomorrow.

He shifted his chair to the side slightly, making space for her to sit.

"Thanks," she murmured as she settled into the chair. A fresh, floral scent swept through the air, and for a brief moment, Will had to steady himself against the unexpected rush of familiarity.

"This place looks great," he said, reaching for a menu from the center of the table. "What's good here?" he asked, hoping to keep the conversation neutral.

"Everything," she said. "But I'm partial to the pumpkin ravioli." She looked at the rest of the table. "With brown butter sage and pine nuts—yum."

"Thanks for the heads-up," Cam said with a dry laugh. He pulled an EpiPen from his bag and slid it into the center of the table. "I always do this, just to let people know I mean business."

"I'd go with the lasagna then," Maya said.

The server took their order, and after drinks were delivered, Shauna clinked her water glass with a butter knife. "Proposing a toast," she said. "Welcome to the team. May this movie be sweet as hot cocoa, with all the perfect mistletoe moments!"

Will swallowed. "Cheers," he eked out. This was really happening. When he turned to see Maya's eyes bright with excitement, he felt even more like the odd man out. All of this—the tinsel, the sappy Christmas love songs, the saccharine and unrealistic dialogue—was fully up Maya's alley. He remembered her in the high school cafeteria at lunchtime, painting her nails with sparkly pink polish. Embroidering flowers on her backpack and decorating her bedroom with posters featuring kittens "hanging in there," the most obnoxiously positive pop songs blaring from her speakers.

And now, here she was, completely in her element, while he—well, he was far from his. One foot in her world, the other still firmly planted in his own, where things were far less...sugary sweet.

He clinked glasses with the crew, then turned to Maya. She flashed him a small, playful grin, her eyes gleaming with that unmistakable spark. "Cheers, Will," she said, her voice warm and confident. "To a great shoot."

"To a great shoot," he echoed, the words tasting a little different on his tongue. Oh boy. This was going to be...interesting.

Maya had expected to feel nervous during the lunch, but twenty minutes in, she was sipping a cocktail and having a great time. The assistant director, Skylar, who was sitting to her left, had read three of Maya's books and was complimentary about her writing style and wanted to know all about Maya's work in progress.

Sitting across from her, Caroline, the production designer, regaled her with stories from the set of one of her favorite made-for-TV movies from the past decade, and about the lengths they had to go to keep the local chipmunks and birds from eating the popcorn strings on the twenty-foot fir tree.

Maya found herself completely absorbed in the conversation—until she caught Will's voice over her shoulder, and like clockwork, she tuned out of her own chat to listen to him. It was a familiar reflex from high school, when she had always hung on his every word. Will had always been thoughtful, funny and kind of philosophical—in that teenage, slightly emo way that, at the time, had somehow seemed cool.

When Caroline got distracted by a ping from her phone, Maya pretended to be occupied by her drink as her focus shifted to Will, who was speaking with one of the producers.

"So you live in New York?" Brent asked.

"I was in Chelsea for the past four years," Will said. "I just moved into a new condo in Bushwick."

Maya took a moment to imagine Will's place. Something sleek and modern, industrial. A record player and stacks of artfully designed albums. A bar cart with aged whiskeys and, soon, a trophy from some film festival on the mantel underneath some kind of indecipherable abstract painting—one of those pieces that, if you were cool enough, you'd *get*. A supermodel perched on a stool at the kitchen island accepting the glass of wine Will poured her after returning to his place following a great dinner date.

She choked on her cocktail at the thought of it, sending a spray of her amber-colored drink across the tablecloth in front of her. She coughed, her eyes watering as the whole table turned to look at her in concern.

"You okay?" said Will.

Maya tried waving them off but the liquid had gone down the wrong way, and she couldn't stop coughing. "Excuse me," she sputtered and stood up from her seat. "I just need a sec."

Will's eyes were filled with concern. "Do you want me to—"

"Nope," said Maya and quickly beelined it to the bathroom.

She closed the door to the single stall and locked it

behind her, coughed a few more times, then stared at herself in the mirror.

"Get a grip," she said. Of course Will had dated many women over the years since they'd been together. Had she thought about it from time to time? Sure. Had she seen the photos of him with them—at premieres, Hollywood parties, all of it? Unfortunately, yes. And while they'd stirred a brief pang of something, it was nothing compared to the wave of jealousy that washed over her now, picturing him with another woman while he sat right beside her, his voice as deep and smooth as ever.

Now, she had to get back out there and get her head on straight and make it through lunch without a single person in the room knowing the effect Will still had on her, even after all these years. "You've got this," she said to herself in the mirror.

She smoothed her hair, straightened her dress and exited the bathroom to find Will standing in the hall.

"They say you shouldn't let someone who's choking go off on their own," he said, his brown eyes soft with concern.

Maya gave him a tight-lipped smile. "And yet, you let me lock myself in the bathroom."

"I could hear you muttering to yourself," he said with a half smile.

Uh-oh.

"Entrees have arrived," Will added, motioning toward the dining room. "Shall we?"

Maya nodded, gathering herself as she followed him back to the table, a strange mix of emotions swirling in her chest.

Shauna had a binder open in front of her when they

reentered the room. Good. They were down to business, and Maya could retreat into being a casual observer instead of a participant.

"First scene is the town square holiday tree decorating," Shauna said to the group. "Call time's six thirty," she said, nodding to Ginger and Blake, "hair and makeup in the trailers. Craft services will be open for six. We've got security overnight, so we won't need to strike the set unless the weather changes, which up until an hour ago, doesn't look like it'll be an issue. We had six fifteen-foot trees delivered yesterday."

"Actually," said Will, looking across the table at Caroline, "I think we'll only need four."

Maya furrowed her eyebrow. She knew exactly the scene they were referencing, where the main characters, Sarah and Ben, attend the town tree-decorating contest. She tried to hold back the words, but they slipped out before she could stop them. "But there were six trees in the story," said Maya. "The fashion tree, the sports tree, the culinary tree, the birds of paradise tree, the Formula One tree, the tree tree—"

"What's a 'tree tree'?" said Will.

Maya paused, caught off guard. "It's meta," she said. "I thought you were into that kind of thing."

Will stared at her for a beat, then turned back to Shauna. "Visually, six will be distracting. Four will be enough."

"We'll get them up later this afternoon," Caroline said. "I'll send you a photo of the setup before dinner."

Will nodded. "Thanks, Caroline."

Maya pursed her lips. Was this the hill she wanted to die on? She took a deep breath and sat back in her chair.

"I had a couple of script notes to share," Will said to the rest of the group, removing his binder from his backpack, which was slung over the back of his chair.

Script notes? Maya eyed him suspiciously, but he just flicked through his pages.

"Page fifty-four," Will said, tracing a finger over the marked-up page. "Sarah tells Ben they didn't have Christmas trees as kids. I want to change that to 'we never had *real* trees as kids.'"

Maya watched as the rest of the table scribbled down their own notes. She struggled to bite her tongue again but couldn't help herself. "But she had no Christmas tree as a kid," she said. "Not just minimal Christmas. That's what makes it such a payoff when her tree wins the prize!"

"It's not realistic, though," said Will. "Her family celebrated Christmas. They weren't rich, but they weren't poor. It makes no sense that they didn't have a tree."

Maya clenched her jaw. Who cared if it didn't make perfect sense? What mattered was the payoff. The more extreme the circumstance, the bigger the payoff. Everyone knew that!

Like of course there was enough room on the plank for Jack at the end of *Titanic*. Rose could for sure have shifted over a little. But how boring would that ending have been? Of course the T. rex in *Jurassic Park* could have outrun the Jeep and not get tired after twenty steps. And did anyone really believe Sam and Annie in *Sleepless in Seattle* could actually meet atop the Empire State Building after a series of so many coincidental events, with perfect timing and dramatic music playing in the background?

It wasn't real life! And that was why people loved it. No one was splitting hairs over the details.

Maya glanced around the room and saw more than one raised eyebrow. It was clear it was time for her to keep her mouth shut.

And she did just that for the remainder of the meeting. Some of what was being discussed flew right over her head—HMI lights, LED panels, soft boxes and the debate over whether boom or lapel mics were the better choice for the first walk-and-talk sequence. But when Cam started outlining the shots he was planning with the crane—an expansive view of Main Street, festooned with twinkling holiday decorations—Maya felt a surge of excitement. She realized that this group of talented professionals was about to turn what had once been a fleeting idea in her mind into a reality for millions to experience.

Surely two fewer trees and one small line change wouldn't be the end of the world, right?

Brent stayed back to take care of the bill while the rest of the group filtered out onto Main Street. They would wait for the production vehicles to take them back to the inn where they were all staying, a ten-minute drive from downtown.

"So we'll meet later on to go over tomorrow's schedule again?" Will said.

"Six o'clock still works for you?" Shauna said. She looked at her watch. "I want to get a run in, then get a good FaceTime in with my kids. They know they won't be seeing much of Mommy over the next couple of weeks."

"Sounds good," said Will. He glanced over Shauna's shoulder to see Maya exiting the restaurant, still chatting with Caroline. It sounded like she was recommending a coffee shop that was good to work at. "And if you need more time, just text me," he said.

"You're not coming back with us?" Shauna asked.

"I'm going to visit my dad," said Will. A printout of the draft listing Hayley had prepared was in his pocket, and hopefully Gene would give the green light without too much of a fuss.

But before that, he wanted to talk to Maya.

He stood on the sidewalk outside the restaurant, pretending to look at something on his phone, and waited as Maya said goodbye to Caroline.

"That's my bakery, right there," he heard her say proudly, and Will glanced up to see Maya pointing down the street.

"Well, you'll have quite the view tomorrow," Caroline said. "That's right where we're setting up."

"I got the pamphlet from the town last week," Maya said. "Road closed to cars. Foot traffic only. I had a few regulars this morning, stocking up for the next few days."

"Hope it doesn't hurt your business too much," Caroline said.

Maya waved it off. "People can walk, or I can deliver. It's all good. I'll be happy to keep an eye on things." She glanced at Will as she said it, her eyes briefly locking with his before quickly shifting away. He raised an eyebrow, and she shot him a half grin—playful, yet defiant—before turning back to Caroline. "Nice to meet you, Caroline. See you tomorrow."

"See you then." Caroline waved at Will before hopping into the van with the rest of the crew, leaving Maya and Will standing alone on the street.

"Nice group of people you'll be working with," said Maya. "Crew is down to earth. And Ginger and Blake don't seem very...diva-ish."

"Most people in the industry are pretty cool," Will said. "Don't believe everything you hear." Maybe he was just stalling his visit to his father's, but he was suddenly desperate to keep her there. Despite her comments challenging his notes in front of the crew, the whole lunch, she'd been fun and dynamic and engaging...like there was golden sparkle dust that existed in the air around her. He'd forgotten how magnetic she was, and it felt good to be by her side. "Do you—do you have time to go for a walk?"

Her expression changed. She looked curious, maybe a bit amused. He waited for her to say yes, but after a moment, she shook her head. "Sorry," she said. "I just got a new puppy, actually. I don't want to leave him more than a couple of hours in his crate at a time."

Will did his best to mask his disappointment. "A new puppy? That's exciting."

"I'll be bringing him to the bakery with me tomorrow," she said. "Feel free to drop in and say hi."

He wasn't getting a walk, but the invitation to see her again tomorrow was something. "All right," he said. "I'll come say hi when I can."

"What are you doing now?" Maya asked. "Hitting up the skate park?"

Will couldn't help but laugh. The skate park was a frequent destination for the students of Sunset County high school after classes, where kids engaged in mildly rebellious behavior like smoking cigarettes and perfecting their ollies, all while trying to look effortlessly cool in their oversize hoodies and worn-out sneakers. "Maybe later this week," he said. "I'm going to go by and see my dad, actually. Then I'll be working back at the hotel."

"You're staying at the Briarwood, right?" Maya asked.

"This week and next," Will said.

Maya nodded in approval. "They're customers of mine. You can try my cheddar scones in the morning."

"Looking forward to that," Will said, although he'd prefer to drive over to the bakery in the early hours, right after opening, and taste one at the source. But he couldn't tell her that. He was in town for two weeks, and he had not just one but two jobs to do.

Seeing Maya was so overwhelmingly nostalgic. Not only did Sunset County feel stuck in time, but being near Maya again brought everything rushing back. It was as if the carefree energy of his teenage years was right there again, that sense that they had all the time in the world to enjoy the present.

And had Maya changed? Outwardly, not much. But there was a marked maturity, a self-assuredness that young Maya hadn't yet grown into, and it was undeniably attractive.

"All right, I guess I'll see you tomorrow," Maya said, adjusting her purse strap. She started to turn to walk away, then stopped. "I still think six Christmas trees are better, to be clear."

"Noted," said Will, enjoying the light challenge in her voice. "Just remember, I'm the movie maker here, right?"

Maya looked back again and rolled her eyes. "Oh, trust me," she said. "That's been made abundantly clear. I don't live under a rock, you know. Bye, Will."

"Bye, Maya," he called. He stood there for a moment,

watching her walk away, a smile tugging at the corner of his lips. Shaking his head, he pulled his keys from his pocket and crossed the street to where his car was parked.

Watching the set take shape against the backdrop of his youth, bringing to life a story from the mind of a woman who still had a hold on him—it felt surreal.

Out of all the places in the world he could be shooting, in all the films he could be working on, how had he ended up back here?

Chapter Six

Gene was napping in the living room when Will arrived at the house, which was silent save for the soft ticking of the grandfather clock on the wall opposite the bay windows. The television was on but muted, the twenty-four-hour news station on screen.

Will went to the kitchen to get a drink and found a note on the table from Agatha. *Gone into town to get some groceries and prescriptions.*

He took a moment to look around the kitchen. The cupboards were tidy and sparsely filled with his dad's staples: instant coffee, rolled oats, cans of soup, microwave popcorn and corn flakes. A calendar from the local Legion hung above the wall-mounted telephone, the only line that Gene could be reached on. The tiling and countertops were dated but clean, Robescarres Lake visible from the open area above the sink.

It wouldn't take long to clear everything out after the place sold. Whoever bought it would have some updating to do, but overall, the place was in great shape, on a section of the lake that was treated to stunning sunsets.

He walked down the hallway past his father's room, which now had a hospital-style bed with some guardrails on the side and a remote control for moving the mattress up to a seated position.

It was strange seeing his father so frail, so vulnerable. Gene Hastings, who used to chop a full cord of firewood in half an hour. Who got up at five o'clock on winter mornings after big storms to shovel not just their driveway but the neighbors' driveways. With a shovel, no less, not a snowblower. *Waste of fossil fuels*, he could still hear Gene say.

Of course a seventy-something-year-old would be expected to lose both muscle and steam over the years, but Will was struck by how quickly his father was deteriorating. It felt as though he was witnessing an accelerated version of the aging process, one that seemed to unfold right before his eyes.

The next door on the left was Will's childhood room, which no longer had his posters hanging or models and movie paraphernalia displayed on the shelves. But the paint on the walls and the furniture was all the same, and it looked like part of the room was now storage for Agatha's medical supplies.

He approached his desk, where he found two shoeboxes and a basket of odds and ends.

"I packed those up for you to look through," Agatha's voice came from behind him. He turned to see her standing in the doorway, holding a bundle of toilet paper in one hand and a package of sponges in the other. "They were at the back of the closet. I think they're all yours."

"They are, thanks, Agatha," he said as she disappeared down the hallway.

The basket held an assortment of old CDs and DVDs, as well as his portable CD player, a small stack of paperback books and an external hard drive, which held who knew how many hours of film that he'd shot during film club in grades eleven and twelve. He'd have to keep that from getting in the wrong hands.

He picked up one of the shoeboxes and carried it to the bed. On top was a folded paper—his valedictorian speech. Another document he'd rather keep under wraps. He set it aside and dug deeper, finding the program for the musical his senior year, *Newsies*. He'd directed the production and worked the light and soundboard, while Maya had practically stolen the show as Katherine Plumber, the reporter with a conscience. It was impossible not to remember how effortlessly she'd lit up the stage.

Under the program was a stack of photos. He was struck, looking through them, by how many moments from his high school years he'd completely forgotten until looking at the images of his young face, those of his friends and, of course, Maya.

Underneath the photos was an old ticket stub. He picked it up and chuckled to himself.

It was the night he'd first kissed Maya, after weeks of pursuing her. She'd finally agreed to go with him to a movie at the Sunset County theater: they were playing *The Covenant*, and he'd never been so happy to be screening such a terrible movie, because it meant that Maya's attention was up for grabs, and when he'd taken her hand in his, she'd looked sideways, and he'd never wanted anything more in his life than to kiss her.

They'd left the theater the moment the credits rolled, and Will bought them both vanilla dip ice cream cones at the truck down by the water. They'd sat with their feet dangling over the edge of the public dock while the ember orange sky darkened to velvet blue. After trading observations on the most cringey parts of the movie, like the waterfall fight scene and the many slow motion walks, they lay back on the wooden planks and sat quietly, looking up at the stars with the sounds of the lake gently lapping against the dock's supporting beams and the far-off sound of music and laughter from a party across the lake.

"Are you going to kiss me already?" Maya finally said, still lying back on the dock, turning to him with a slight smile on her face. "I'm getting impatient."

"I'm the one who's waited all year for you to agree to go out with me," Will said, propping himself up on one elbow and gazing down at her. "So I know something about patience."

"Has it been worth it?" Maya said.

"Oh yes," said Will, brushing a strand of hair from her face before dipping down and meeting her lips with his.

They'd made out on the dock until a water taxi transporting some guests from the party across the lake approached with its headlights on. Rather than waiting to see the curious faces of people who knew very well they'd interrupted something, Will had taken Maya's hand and led her back to the theater, where they picked up his bike. He'd walked her home to the small bungalow, a ten-minute walk from town.

He'd kissed her good night—this time a little more chastely, in case Mr. or Mrs. Monroe happened to be watching from inside—and as he rode his bike home through the warm evening air, the world felt alight with possibility.

Will placed the ticket on top of the pile of items, and before he closed the shoebox, he noticed a glittery gold piece of cardboard nestled to one side. He pulled it out and turned it over in his hand, a pang of regret hitting him right in the chest.

Shine bright in LA, Maya's familiar scrawl read on the back. *I love you.*

She'd given it to him on their last night together in Sunset County, sitting out on that same dock where they'd had their first kiss, their feet dangling in the water. He was due to fly out in the morning and was fresh off a blowout fight with Gene, who'd clearly still held on to hope that Will was just calling his bluff about this whole "California nonsense," as he called it.

Will had wondered if Gene might relent and at least drive him to the airport, but instead, he'd be taking the bus down to the city, with his suitcase and a heart full of disappointment.

Holding Maya in his arms down by the water, he'd experienced a hint of something deep down that things weren't going to work with them but couldn't bring himself to express his fear. Instead, he ignored the feeling and gazed up at the sky, wishing things could be different between him and his father.

Will remembered tucking the card in his shoebox that night. Maya's wide-eyed optimism for their future had made him feel like a complete fraud, and he couldn't bring himself to put it in his suitcase.

She'd seen such a bright future for them. And he'd let her down.

When he returned to the living room, Gene was awake, staring ahead at the television. He glanced at

Will when he entered the room, then back at the new program. "Can you believe what this idiot government is doing to the economy?" Gene said. "Kicking the debt can down the street for some other government to deal with in the future. Writing blank checks. Who voted for these people? Doesn't anyone know that printing money causes inflation?"

Will chuckled, then settled in on the couch. If he didn't know any better, he'd think his dad's mind was as sharp as ever. But he'd been uttering those same phrases, or variations thereof, for decades however, so maybe this was just him speaking out of habit.

"I ordered delivery from Pete's Pies," Will said. "Hope that's all right."

"Is that another new place in town?" Gene said, still distracted by the television screen.

"They've been there for years, Dad," he said. "Best pie in Sunset County."

Gene grunted, then grabbed the remote to turn up the volume on the television and dropped it on the ground.

Will jumped up to grab it off the carpet, but Gene waved him away. "I've got it, I've got it," he said. "I wish people would stop treating me like I'm some kind of invalid."

Will watched for a moment as Gene bent over in his chair, feeling for the remote. "Here, Dad, just let me get it," he said. He picked up the device and placed it in his dad's hand. "*Jeopardy*'s on. Want to change the channel?"

Gene paused. "Which one again?"

"Channel eight." Gene pressed a button, and the opening theme to *Jeopardy* filled the room just as the doorbell rang.

"Right on time," said Will. "I'll grab some plates and be right back."

Will joined Agatha at the door and pressed some cash in the delivery boy's hand. "Want to join us for a bite?" Will asked Agatha.

"I'm going to head home for a few minutes if that's okay," said Agatha. "My daughter is visiting with my granddaughter."

"How old's your granddaughter?" Will said.

"Just turned ten." Agatha shook her head. "They just found out little Kaley needs to get these expensive braces to fix her teeth. We're just going to sit down together and make a savings plan to make it happen. My daughter changed jobs last year and doesn't have benefits until she passes the one-year mark."

Will nodded. "I hope now that my dad's moving into the home, you're still going to have work."

"Don't you worry about me," Agatha said. "There's no shortage of work around here. I'll have another client the day after Mr. Hastings moves."

Will nodded. "Take your time," he said. "I'm happy to stick around."

"I'll come back to help him get ready for bed," said Agatha. "What time should I be back?"

He felt badly making such a short visit, especially since he still had to show his dad the listing that he was hoping would go up in a couple of days. He'd move his meeting with Shauna back. "I've got a meeting at six. But I can push it back. Seven thirty?" He felt additionally guilty that he wouldn't have the slightest idea how to help his father get ready for bed. Not that his father would want Will to see him in any kind of vulnerable situation anyway.

"See you then. And, Will," Agatha said, pausing. "I'm not saying you are. But in case you're feeling conflicted by any of this…you're doing the right thing. I've worked with many individuals in the same situation as your father. And as hard as it is to see it, his progression is happening quickly. The transition will be easier for him if he's still overall aware and understanding of what's happening. It was good of you to come out and do this."

"Of course," said Will, but he was suddenly hit with a pang of guilt that it took a health concern of this magnitude for him to come back to be with his father. Even though she was being complimentary, he was sure that inside, Agatha probably thought he was a total deadbeat son.

She smiled and squeezed his elbow. "I'll see you at seven thirty."

Will texted Shauna to let her know he was delayed, then brought the pizza box to the living room with a couple of plates and some napkins.

By the time Agatha returned, Will was more than ready to leave again. Dinner had been good—Gene had eaten a piece of pizza and answered a couple of *Jeopardy* questions, which was good to see, but by the time Will pulled out the listing and tried to get his father to give his blessing, Gene was either pretending not to hear him or the idea of moving out had put him in what seemed like a trance.

Will bid Gene and Agatha farewell and drove back to the Briarwood. Agatha's words echoed in his mind as he pulled his car into a parking spot. *You're doing the right thing.*

Before he got out of the car, he texted Hayley. Good to go with the listing tomorrow morning, he typed.

No use delaying the inevitable.

Chapter Seven

"Come on, baby," Maya cooed at Bruce. He was being such a good boy and standing still while she clipped his blue harness around his tiny body, then fastened his leash.

There was a ninety-nine percent chance she'd be carrying him for most of the walk to the bakery, but slowly but surely, they'd practice, and in a few weeks' time, he'd be a champion walker.

Sure enough, as they exited her house, and she led him down the path toward the sidewalk, Bruce made a hard right turn onto the grass and started sniffing a fallen pine cone.

"Okay, okay," Maya said, scooping up all eight pounds of him and cradling him in her arms like a baby. "You get chauffeur service today."

When she turned the corner, Main Street was still dark and quiet save for a security guard sitting on a camping chair near the set. Under the dim streetlights, Maya could see the four giant trees standing in the middle of the street, festooned with colorful decorations and surrounded by a gate made of wooden candy canes. Several of the streetlamps had giant wreaths hanging from them.

Maya was tempted to go over and look at everything

up close, but she couldn't get distracted. There would be plenty of time later to take everything in under the glow of the spotlights, with the cast on set.

"Here we are," she said, after unlocking the bakery door and flicking on the lights. She placed Bruce on the ground and let him sniff around for a bit. The new smells were likely putting him into sensory overload. "Welcome to your new home away from home."

She kept an eye on him while she flicked on some music, then started about her daily prep. She set her workstations, lined trays with parchment, mixed and kneaded dough, prepared fillings and glazes and started to slide trays in the ovens.

He got underfoot a couple of times—she'd have to be careful when carrying hot trays—and he barked every time a timer went off, but it was nice to have his presence in the bakery while she was working.

Around five thirty, some action started to materialize outside the bakery. The generators for the white trucks, which had been parked overnight, turned on, sending a gentle vibration through the space. Crew members passed the window, prompting Bruce to freak out. She brought him to the back and coaxed him into Minnie's old kennel. "Just for a while, sweetie, while Mommy gets everything ready for the day."

He let out a light series of cries of discontent.

Maya continued her prep, and as the sun came up, the street continued to fill with a flurry of activity. She had to remind herself to focus and not give into the temptation to watch as slowly, the lights turned on and Main Street was transformed into what she imagined the Warner Brothers backlot looked like.

Cassie entered the bakery, the entrance bells jingling. "Long time no see!" she said. Bruce yapped from behind the counter. "And there's a new baker in town."

"My new assistant," Maya said. "Although he really needs to work on his piping skills, or I—" Maya stopped. "Wait. Has Lucas found a job yet?"

Cassie shook her head. "The only place willing to take him was the Hidden Oar, but quite frankly I don't need him working at a bar until all hours of the night."

"What about all hours of the morning?" Maya said. "I could really use some help. But it would mean arriving at around five o'clock. Would he be interested in working for a couple of hours before school?"

Cassie's eyes widened. "Really?" she said. "That would be kind of perfect. He'd have to go to bed early instead of staying up all night playing video games. And working here, he'd learn something useful."

"I'll have him turning out some top-notch baguettes in no time," Maya said. "I can only pay minimum wage—"

"At this point, I would pay you to have him," said Cassie. "Let's just say grade twelve hasn't started off with quite the bang I was hoping for."

"Why don't you talk to him after school, and if he wants to come by sometime this week, we can chat." Maya's gaze shifted over Cassie's shoulder. "I'm thinking of staying open a little later this week until the filming wraps for the day. Lots of curious people out who might end up dropping in while they're here."

"It must be so exciting to see your book brought to life! And I'm sure you'll get some extra foot traffic, with all of Sunset County out to see the show," said Cassie.

Maybe. But Maya was interested in more than a few

extra sales. After the exterior scenes were wrapped, she'd have to figure out a way to weasel her way on set to keep an eye on the interior scenes.

"I'll take a loaf of the multigrain," said Cassie. "Sliced, please."

"Sure thing."

When Maya brought the bread back to the counter, Cassie was craning her neck to see out the front window. "I won't lie… I'm hoping to get a glimpse of Blake O'Connor. And I heard the director could be a Hollywood star himself."

"Don't say that too loud," Maya said. "The last thing Will Hastings needs is an ego boost."

"Oh, that's right, I heard he grew up here," Cassie said. She tapped her debit card on the machine. "You know him?"

"Used to," said Maya. She pulled off the receipt and handed it to Cassie, but she waved it away.

"Okay, if I can get Lucas to come by after school, I will," she said. "Something tells me he'll be here. I told him he's not getting any allowance until he pulls his average into the B territory, and I think he's getting sick of bringing his own lunch to school while all his friends are eating pizza and french fries from the cafeteria."

"Whatever lights a fire under you, right?"

"Exactly," Cassie said. "Thanks, Maya, see you soon."

Bruce had settled in his kennel, so Maya took the opportunity to prop the bakery door open and watch the goings-on from the entrance.

She took out her phone and snapped a shot of the other side of Main Street, which looked even more like someone had blasted it with a Christmas confetti gun since she'd arrived in the morning: the set department had covered the lampposts in garland and twinkly lights. She squinted to see that the bookstore's window display was dressed with holiday books, with silver snowflakes hanging, and Rise and Grind's door had a big fat wreath hanging from it.

She silently cursed herself for forgetting the coffee shop was closed for the morning—she remembered Shauna saying something at the lunch meeting about them getting the exterior shots of Ginger and Blake exiting the shop with their hot drinks before the tree scene—the inside shoot was on Wednesday. Normally, Maya would take over their order of biscotti and pick up her coffee right before they both opened. She'd have to find a place to get her second coffee. Maybe craft services would let her grab something.

A set of what looked like train tracks was set up, zippering down the middle of Main Street, and two men were testing running a moving camera along it.

And there was Will, standing at a screen, wearing jeans, a hoodie and a baseball cap, talking with Shauna and pointing at something on the screen. Maya studied his face. He looked thoughtful but serious. Her pulse quickened slightly at the thought that he was thinking deeply about something related to her story.

Her story. She took a deep breath in and allowed herself to enjoy the moment. Will might have been the last person she would have picked to direct her movie, but the day had finally come.

She was going to savor it.

But in the meantime, she thought, as she saw her next customer approaching, she had some baked goods to move. The yin to Edith Campbell's yang of Sunset County's most dynamic duo was Margaret Anderson. The two women had moved in together after both of their husbands' passing. Maya smiled to herself as she watched Mrs. Anderson, whose feisty spirit and sequined jacket didn't quite align with her age.

Mrs. Anderson pulled her grocery cart up over the curb. "Morning, Maya!" she called, grinning her pink-lipsticked smile.

"Good morning, Mrs. Anderson," she said. "How are you today?"

"Just fine," she said, looking Maya up and down. "Now look at you! Are you all dressed up and ready to step on the scene?"

Maya followed her into the bakery. "Oh, this old thing?" she said, gesturing toward her favorite marigold peasant dress, something she'd never once worn to work before this day. "Just a regular day!"

Had she gotten up a little earlier than usual to apply her makeup more carefully and style her hair so that after she finished baking, she could let it free from her hairnet to fall nicely around her shoulders instead of piling it up on top of her head for the rest of the day? Maybe. But no one needed to know that.

She half listened to Mrs. Anderson talk about some kind of sewing bee coming up at the community center and her Friday line dancing with Knox Walker. "He's such a dreamboat, our Knox!" Mrs. Anderson said, laughing.

"Too bad Andie Carter snapped him up before you had your chance," Maya said, which elicited a hoot from Mrs. Anderson. "We'll have to find you another beau."

"Couldn't be happier for those two," Mrs. Anderson said. "And what's this I hear about you being our special guest at book club on Wednesday?"

Maya grinned. "I can't wait," she said. "There are only a few people I'd stay up past my bedtime for. And the ladies of the book club are all on that list."

Maya looked over Mrs. Anderson's shoulder to see Ginger Estrada and Blake O'Connor arriving on set. Ginger was wearing a beautiful crimson colored coat that tied at the waist, and looked every bit as down-to-earth with a touch of glamour as Maya had written her in the book. Blake was more casual—good—Ben was meant to be a foil for Sarah's big-city style, and the wardrobe department had hit the mark with a parka and blue jeans. The man wore them well.

Mrs. Anderson turned and followed her gaze. "Speaking of dreamboats!" She let out a wolf whistle. "Edith and I are planning to come back this afternoon with our lawn chairs and watch the movie shoot," she said. "Maybe we'll bring some popcorn!"

Maya grinned. "I'm making some caramel popcorn balls later this morning, actually," she said. "Want me to put some aside for you?"

"You bet," said Mrs. Anderson. "I'll see you later, Maya."

Maya wiped a few crumbs off the counter with a dish towel and peered into Bruce's crate. "What do you think, sweetie?" she said. "Should we take a walk over and see what's going on?"

Bruce let out a yip.

"I'll take that as a yes," she said, plucking her coat from the hook beside the pantry and shrugging it over her shoulders. She clipped Bruce onto his leash, hung up her Back in Ten sign and exited the shop into the Christmas wonderland, the warm October sun now shining overhead.

The breeze blowing through the monitor bay was warm, but the only thing the screen in front of him was displaying was nine by twelve inches of in-your-face Christmas schmaltz.

Will had only been on set for ninety minutes, and he'd already uttered the words *poinsettia*, *mittens* and *evergreen*, and somehow, the sleeve of his sweatshirt was inexplicably covered in red glitter.

This is your life for only three weeks, he reminded himself, and took a deep, steadying breath. It was going to be okay. But if things continued at this rate, he might need to book a mid-December flight to Bora Bora, park himself at a beachside canteen and skip Christmas altogether.

But now he needed to focus on the task at hand. One hundred percent pure holiday romance magic. The perfect shot of Ginger and Blake, a.k.a. Sarah and Ben, strolling arm in arm, falling in love under the glow of the white string lights.

"Let's slow that down just a bit," Will called. "We're strolling, not charging, all right?"

Ginger nodded. Her arm was laced in Blake's, and Will wanted to catch all the details in the background, which, he had to give it to Caroline, read spectacularly on screen as the couple did a walk-and-talk.

He gave a thumbs-up to Skylar, who returned the gesture with a quick nod. Her eyes widened. "Hold for sound," Skylar called, her strong voice carrying over the set. "And we're rolling in three, two..." She motioned the one count without saying it out loud, and it was on.

The first shot of the movie always gave Will a thrill, even though nine times out of ten it would end up on the cutting room floor.

He watched the screen as Ginger and Blake, big smiles plastered on their faces, started to walk, Cam and the camera operator slowly moving the camera down the dolly tracks ahead of them. They looked good. More than good. And Cam was capturing the moment with precision.

It was rare to get a perfect first take. Actors needed to get warmed up, camera angles needed adjusting. Sometimes he couldn't see the perfect vision for a shot until it was playing out in front of him, and an idea for something better materialized in his mind.

So, it surprised him, watching through the monitor, to see Ginger and Blake hit their marks perfectly, deliver their dialogue without any hesitation, and he had to admit, convincingly.

"All right, cut," he said. "That was...great."

Skylar must have noticed the surprise in his voice. She sidled up beside him and spoke quietly. "These guys are pros. They're used to quick shoots. No time to mess up your lines or get precious with the shots."

Will nodded. "Let's roll again," he said, if only to assuage his own fear that surely, he was missing something.

Two minutes later, he was calling cut on another perfect take. Was he dreaming?

"All right," he said. "Let's get the close-ups." He looked at Skylar. "Nice work," he said.

She smiled, satisfied.

The hair and makeup artist stepped onto set, gently tapping some powder onto Ginger's nose as the gaffers swiftly moved the camera onto a tripod. They were prepping to capture Ginger and Blake delivering their same dialogue again, but in a tighter shot from the chest up.

It would be a few minutes before they were ready to start rolling again, enough time to get a coffee. He made his way to the craft services truck and noticed Maya exiting Flour Child, a little puppy not much bigger than an oversize squirrel by her side.

His eyes flitted over her yellow dress which cut off right above the knee, and her brown suede boots and jean jacket. Her hair ran loose and glossy down her back, and he watched as she slid on a pair of oversize sunglasses, then looked both ways down Main Street before noticing him.

He gave her a quick wave, then glanced over to see how close to being ready they were for the next shot. Cam was still fiddling with the tripod. He had a couple minutes.

Will made his way toward Maya, unable to resist teasing her. "Are you sure you adopted a puppy?" he called out. "That looks more like a stuffed animal than a living, breathing creature."

"He's very much alive, actually," Maya said, scooping him up and presenting him to Will. "This is Bruce."

Will reached out and scratched the puppy lightly behind the ears. "Cute," he said. He glanced up at Maya, who was looking at Bruce with all the love in the world. "Any acting experience? We're looking for a few more pups for the 'rein-dog parade.'" He made quotation marks with his fingers as he said it.

Maya's eyebrow shot up immediately. "Not yet," she said. "And I'm not sure I like your tone. The rein-dog parade is a very serious parade. And a fan favorite chapter of the book, I should add. I hope it gets the attention it deserves." She deposited Bruce back on the ground, then fixed him in her gaze. "And as Bruce's agent, I'd be happy to discuss a daily rate. But he requires some specialty items at the craft table."

"Speaking of which," Will said, looking over at the craft services table, which was set up under the awning beside Rise and Grind. "I was about to grab a coffee. Then I have to get back on set." He paused for a moment as a gaffer passed with a light stand. "Can I get you something?"

Maya paused, and her expression shifted. "I'll take a coffee, if you're offering," she said. "Thanks." A gentle breeze blew some strands of hair into her face, and he imagined how soft they must feel as she tucked them behind her ear.

"Will, we're ready," Skylar called from the monitor bay.

He gave Skylar a thumbs-up, then motioned to a production assistant who was standing a few feet away next to a pylon. "Hey," he said to the kid, "can you show Maya here to the craft table? And if you don't mind, I'd love a coffee in a few minutes, too. Black, please," he said. As a rule, he preferred to get his own drinks, but the kid had looked bored out of his skull until the moment Will made the request. "See you, Maya," he said. "Bruce."

Maya trailed the production assistant while Will rejoined Shauna at the monitor, checking the framing of the shot. "All right, everyone in position," he called. "We're rolling."

The rest of the morning went smoothly, other than a missing toque from the costume department for one of the town carolers and a brief spell of time when the wind picked up, and they had to improvise a screen to keep Ginger's hair from blowing in her mouth and getting stuck in her thick lip gloss as she delivered her lines.

By noon, they'd broken for lunch and were about to move over to Rise and Grind for the next setup. Will noticed a small crowd of Sunset County residents had gathered to watch the filming.

"You should probably go over at some point and say hello," Shauna said, approaching with her clipboard in hand. "Looks like you've got some fans out."

Sure enough, there was an older man holding a poster of *Auto Toon*, and a couple both in red berets, a nod to one of his first films about the French resistance during World War II.

"There's something I need to do first," Will said. "I'll be back in twenty. Enjoy your lunch."

After making a quick stop at the catering table, he crossed the street and turned right into the alley behind the businesses lining Main Street. He made his way past the garbage cans and the parked cars until the scent of sugar and fresh bread grew stronger. Toward the end of the alley, the bakery door was propped open by a small wooden block edged in the doorframe.

Will rapped on the steel door a few times.

Seconds later, Maya appeared.

"I brought you another coffee," Will said, extending

the paper cup to her. "As an apology for closing down Rise and Grind for a couple days."

A small smile spread across Maya's lips. "Thank you," she said. "And personal delivery. What a nice touch." She held the cup in salute, then took a small sip. "Mmm," she said. "I just took something out of the oven that will go perfectly with this. Want to come in?"

"I've got to be back in ten. But sure," he said. He followed her into the bakery's kitchen, which smelled of a mixture of rising yeast and caramel. The Supremes played over the speakers, and in the corner, Bruce sniffed through the slats of his kennel.

"Here," said Maya, sliding something from a cooling rack onto a paper napkin. "Have it now. It's the perfect temperature."

He accepted the napkin, which held a piece of shortbread, and indeed, he could feel the warmth through the thin paper. He took a bite, the sweet buttery cookie crumbling in his mouth perfectly. "Good grief," he said, after chewing and swallowing. "This tastes like heaven."

Maya grinned. "Keeps 'em coming back for more," she said. "Although with the price of butter these days, I'm just about breaking even on those."

"You could charge double whatever it is you're charging right now, and I'm sure people would pay," said Will.

Maya wiped her hands on her apron, broke a piece off one of the cookies and popped it in her mouth. "I'm not out to gouge anyone," she said, after she'd chewed and swallowed. "Want another?"

"Yes, but I'll leave those for the residents of Sunset County to enjoy," he said. "We're filming the tree lighting later this afternoon."

"With six trees, right?" she asked.

"Four," he said firmly. "I'd better go. Bye, Maya."

He didn't even need to ask if he'd see her again later. That glint in her eye told him that despite the fact that she was playing nice for the moment, she'd be watching over the set like a hawk.

Chapter Eight

It was just after five o'clock when they were reviewing blocking for the final scene of their call sheet for the day. It was the moment when Sarah and Ben were standing with the rest of the community to count down from ten, and the trees would alight to the delight of the crowd. Now that the sun had disappeared behind the buildings on the west side of the street, there were no shadows to contend with, so they could cheat the evening scene with greater ease.

Stu was giving directions to the extras, and Will chuckled to himself hearing the gruff guy tell one of them that she could stand to be "a little more delighted" when the lights finally turned on. Cam was changing up a lens, and Blake and Ginger were running their lines one last time before they rolled.

Will's attention drifted momentarily back down the street toward Flour Child, where Maya was flipping the sign in the window to Closed. She stepped outside with Bruce in tow, locking the door behind her. When she saw him, she gave a small wave.

Will waved back, his thoughts briefly pulling away from the set before Skylar's voice cut through the air: "All right, we're prepped to roll in five!"

He snapped back into work mode, his focus zeroing in on the scene unfolding before him. Time to get back to business.

He had to cut halfway through the first take when only two of the four trees lit up. The second take was better, but Stu still wasn't happy with the background actors' performance, so to humor the man, Will rolled again.

"This time let's get Ben to plug the lights in instead," Will said. "Blake, can you keep that kind of deadpan look on your face until the big moment, then just give me the sense that you're actually slightly impressed?"

"Got it," said Blake, accepting the power cord that Ginger handed him.

"Everyone ready?" Will asked.

"Wait!" a voice called out from the stanchions separating the set from the sideway.

Will turned to see Maya, a look of indignation on her face. "What?" he said. "Maya, we're just about to roll."

"But Ben can't plug the lights in!" she said. "It's been the mayor's job since the competition started!"

"Maya," he started.

"Part of the reason Garrison Creek is so popular at Christmas is because of tradition. You can't go inventing new procedures. It doesn't make any sense!"

"I thought it didn't have to make sense to be good," Will said.

Maya pursed her lips. "It shouldn't be Ben plugging in the trees."

Will felt the crew staring at him. This had gone too far. "Take five, everyone," he said. He marched over to Maya and spoke under his breath. "Maya," he said, doing his best to keep his tone measured. The crew members nearby were trying their best to look busy, but he could feel their eyes on him. "I'd like to discuss this with you in private."

Maya blinked. Her expression was playful, but he knew better. "What's there to discuss?"

She could feign innocence all she wanted. But they were going to have a conversation.

"Follow me," he muttered through gritted teeth.

"Fine," she replied with a casual shrug. "I'm in no rush."

He checked his walkie as he led her to the office to make sure he was avoiding a hot mic situation.

The temporary production office was set up in an empty storefront they'd taken over for the duration of the shoot where they'd set up a couple of desks, and where they could store some set items and some of the more expensive gear overnight, rather than leave it in the production trailer.

He held the door open for her and caught the faint scent of her perfume, soft and alluring as she breezed by. Her face wore a light smile of—what was it? Satisfaction? Victory? Whatever it was, it irked him, even though it was so damn pretty he could have made himself forget his annoyance.

Will closed the door and flicked the latch to lock. This would be quick, and he didn't want any interruptions.

"Maya," he said, his gaze locking on to hers, "I understand you have a vested interest in this project."

"And?" she said, raising an eyebrow, her gaze never breaking with his.

"And while your...suggestions are appreciated—"

"Are they, though?" Maya said, her voice dripping

with playful mockery. She batted her eyelashes a couple of times. "Because a few minutes ago, you seemed to be going a shade of red that matched Ginger's peacoat."

"I was not," Will said. "But I will kindly ask you to reserve your opinions to share when we're not right in the middle of a take. This production schedule is tight. We need to move forward with our plan, and our plan doesn't include changing dialogue or plot points on the fly."

"Well, I wouldn't really use the word *change*," Maya said, taking a step forward, a challenging but incredibly sexy expression on her face. Her voice was low and smooth and awoke something in him.

"What would you call it then?" he challenged.

"I'd call it...return to former glory." He could tell by the way she was looking at him with one eyebrow raised that she wanted a reaction out of him.

Will couldn't help but scoff. "Come on. You think you know better than I do how to make a movie?"

Her lips turned up in that same teasing smile. "You think you can tell a better love story than me?"

"Movies and books are completely different media," Will countered. "If we included every last detail from your story, the movie would be twenty hours long. And trust me, it would be boring."

Maya's eyes widened. "Boring?" she said, incredulously. "Did you just call my story *boring*?"

Will let out a heavy sigh, frustration creeping into his voice. "No, I didn't say your story's boring, I—"

"But you think it's stupid," she interrupted, her tone sharp.

His eyes snapped to hers. "What? When did I ever say that?"

"You didn't have to say it," Maya said. Her gaze was intense and unyielding as she took another confident step closer. "It's in your tone of voice every time you discuss a plot point or give one of the actors direction. You think I didn't notice how you were dripping with sarcasm when you asked Blake to 'fix her in a more loving glare'? I thought you were going to choke on your words!"

Now his blood was boiling. But there was something else, something that had nothing to do with this argument. The way she stood there, fearless, unafraid to tell him exactly what was on his mind, her lips just inches from his. The way she looked at him as though she could read every thought in his head. At the same time as he wanted her to stop talking, he wanted to run his fingers through her soft, flowing hair and pull her gorgeous body tight against his and kiss the sharpness right out of her words.

"I want you to stay away from the set tomorrow," Will said.

Maya's jaw tightened. "I work across the street. And don't forget you're filming at *my bakery* on Thursday."

He was going to have to speak with Shauna about that one. Could they shift it to another location? The last thing he needed was to feel beholden to Maya for shutting down her business for the day. She seemed confident enough to make whatever demands she wanted already.

"Can we make an agreement," Will said, choosing his words carefully, "that if you want to provide feedback on anything that's happening on set, that you do so quietly and sparingly, and you do it though Shauna? I can't afford any more interruptions."

A tense quiet hung in the air as Maya's eyes searched

his. When she finally spoke, her voice was surprisingly calm. "Fine," she said. "I'll agree to that."

He hadn't expected her to give in so easily.

"But on one condition," she said.

There it was. The condition he knew was coming, that would make his life more complicated than it always was.

"Bruce gets to be in the rein-dog parade."

Will raised an eyebrow. "Your untrained puppy?" he said. "If that's not a recipe for disaster, I don't know what it is."

"You brought it up earlier."

"I was kidding."

"All right, it's up to you," Maya said, shrugging nonchalantly. "Because as far as I can tell, the set isn't locked down or anything. Anyone can stand close by and watch what's going on."

Will let out a frustrated sigh. "Fine," he said. "Bruce can have a part. And you're going to keep your distance."

"Fine." Maya's lips turned up in a delicious grin. "He's going to be a star," she said. "And by the way, I noticed that none of those trees has a star on them. What kind of Christmas tree doesn't have a star?"

Before he could respond, Maya stepped closer, her body almost flush with his. He could feel the heat of her presence, the magnetic attraction pulsing in the air between them. She placed a single finger on his chest, right above where he could feel his heart racing.

"Oh and, Maya," said Will. She wanted to be coquettish, playful? Two could play at that game. "You know, you don't have to be worried about this film being excellent. I don't do anything unless I go all in."

"I hope that's true," she murmured, just as a knock

came at the trailer door. She slowly pulled her finger away and stepped back, and Will did his best to mask the fact that he was taking a deep breath in. "Because you might have years of credits ahead of you. But this might be my first and last. And it has to be perfect."

Chapter Nine

Despite herself, Maya managed to stay well away from the set all day on Tuesday. She busied herself by making some of the fondant pieces for the Snow White cake that could be refrigerated in advance: a red apple with glossy glaze to give it a slight shine, blue birds molded to sit delicately on top of the cake, a queen's crown with sparkling golden dust and the birthday girl's two favorite dwarves, Sleepy and Bashful. All she would need to do on Saturday morning was bake the vanilla base of the cake and frost it with vanilla icing, then place the fondant pieces in the right spots with some piping here and there.

She spent any other lulls playing with Bruce and his chew toy and trying to lay the groundwork for some basic commands: sit, paw, stay, heel. He liked the treats but didn't so much like the directions.

The day flew by, and while Maya was tempted to walk by the set after closing up the shop, she kept to her word and took a left toward home rather than meandering down Main Street after locking up.

On Wednesday, Maya wasn't feeling as obedient. She wanted to be back in the action, and there was no denying that replaying what had happened between her and

Will in the production office wasn't as good as the real thing. She wanted to see him again.

She'd bothered him in more ways than one, she knew that for sure. And the whole thing had left her with a current of electricity that burned bright until late in the evening, far after the time when she should have been asleep for the greatest chance at waking up with a reasonable head on her shoulders.

If she wanted anywhere near back on set again, she was going to have to show more deference. Be a team player. So it was on her to smooth things over.

You catch more flies with honey, Maya thought to herself as she grabbed a metal bowl from the bakery's top shelf. As far as she could remember, Will loved nothing more in the world than a classic chocolate chip cookie. She could bring a warm batch to set, and surely the craft services people would let her linger around a little. The cookies would double as a peace offering and a reason for her to take a peek at what was going on inside Rise and Grind.

She creamed the butter with the sugar and measured out some almond flour—it retained moisture better than all-purpose flour, for a chewier, melt-in-your-mouth texture—added the eggs, vanilla, baking soda, chips and a light sprinkling of salt.

After mixing the dough and forming twenty-four perfect balls, spaced evenly apart on two cookie sheets, she slid the cookies into the oven, set the timer and did some tidying up while she waited.

After the cookies baked—perfectly, she noted—she allowed them just enough time to cool, then slid them onto a silver tray she kept to display free samples every now and then, then hung her Back in Ten sign on the door.

"I won't be long, sweetie," she said to Bruce. She would prefer to bring him, but there was no need for her to give anyone another reason to ask her to leave set.

There was a craft services table set up outside of Rise and Grind, just close enough that she'd be able to get a peek inside the coffee shop.

She approached the table, where a woman in a hot pink trucker hat and surly expression sat scrolling through her phone. She barely looked up at Maya.

"Hi, I'm Maya," she said. "I'm the writer of the book this movie is based on."

The woman glanced up with a look that confirmed that whatever she was looking at on her phone was infinitely more impressive.

"I brought these for the crew," Maya said, smiling. "Mind if I leave them here?"

"Go for it," said the woman. "Tatum's in charge of catering. She had to go get more ice from the grocery store. I'm just here to make sure no one swipes anything."

Excellent, thought Maya. Unlike Tatum, whom she'd met the day before and who watched her catering table like a hawk, refilling any item someone plucked within seconds, this woman might as well be a cardboard cutout meant to scare away the local birds: the woman clearly had no interest in managing any aspect of the set.

Maya placed the cookies on the table, gave the woman her most winning grin, then edged closer to the door. Most of the action inside was blocked by equipment, but she could make out Blake and Ginger sitting across from one another at a table, mugs in front of them. Ginger's hair was being fussed over, and Blake was reviewing his lines.

Someone must have said something about starting to roll soon. Maya watched as people took their places, the actors straightened their backs and shifted their expressions, and in the background, Skylar counted down with her fingers.

Blake and Ginger were a perfect Ben and Sarah. If she could only hear them deliver their lines. She edged just a little closer to the window and glanced over to see if Trucker Hat cared at all that she was there, but the woman was lost in her phone.

When Maya looked back, there was some activity on set. All of a sudden, the door in front of her swung open, and members of the crew started to file out.

Uh-oh. Maya turned to leave, but before she could slip away, she heard her name.

Argh. It was Will.

"You're not supposed to be here," said Will.

She turned to find him standing right behind her, an expression of annoyance in his eyes, and something else. Amusement?

"I just wanted to bring these cookies for everyone," said Maya. "To apologize. They're still warm..." she said, noting the slight shift in his expression. "Chocolate chip. Your favorite."

"So this didn't have anything to do with you wanting to be on set?" Will said. "After you agreed to keep your distance?"

She shook her head. "Definitely not."

He glanced over at the plate of cookies.

She picked it up and held it up toward his face. There was no way he'd be able to resist that scent.

"Thank you," Will said.

He was about to say something else when Cam and Caroline exited the coffee shop.

"Just baked," said Maya, holding out the plate.

"Ooo, and still warm," said Caroline, picking one off the plate. Cam grabbed one, too, and they continued on their way, leaving Maya and Will alone again.

Will took a bite and raised an eyebrow.

"Apology accepted?" Maya said.

"I'll think about it," said Will, as a voice came over his walkie. He slid it from his belt loop. "I guess you're on your way now?"

"Yep," she said. She didn't need to tell him she'd be back in fifteen minutes to pick up her plate.

"What's the ETA on the set change?" he said into the walkie. A garbled staticky voice sounded in return, so Maya waved and mouthed goodbye. Will held up the cookie in salute with the walkie up to his ear, then disappeared back through the door onto set.

Maya could see a customer outside of Flour Child, so she left her detecting post and hurried back to the bakery.

"Sorry!" she called to the woman, whom Maya recognized as a long-time cottager over on Robescarres Lake.

The woman ordered a dozen sesame rolls and a small carrot cake, then put in an order for a whiskey-barrel-themed Jack Daniels cake for her husband's retirement party in two weeks. They talked through a few details, and the woman shared some photos of a cake she'd seen online.

"I'll make it even better than that," Maya said with a wink.

"No doubt," the woman said. "I've seen your creations from the party center's Instagram. Amazing!"

"I appreciate that," Maya said, then allowed the compliment to sit. She *was* good at what she did. The bakery was thriving, and her cakes regularly racked up thousands of likes on Instagram. The nagging feeling of inadequacy she had been battling these last few days—something she hadn't experienced in a long time—wasn't a reflection of her abilities. It was just the shadow cast by Will and his overwhelming success.

She couldn't let him make her feel like she wasn't enough again.

After the woman left, Maya spent a few minutes jotting down some notes for the cake. She only looked up when the red and blue lights of a passing paramedic van down Main Street flashed through the front window.

Maya dropped her pen on her notebook and approached the entrance, watching as the vehicle pulled up across from Rise and Grind. A team of two paramedics exited the vehicle and pulled a couple of bags from the back of the van. A production assistant waved them down from the entrance to the coffee shop.

She flipped the sign again, locked the bakery door and jogged toward the set, hanging back far enough to be respectful but close enough to figure out what was going on.

"Is everything okay in there?" Maya asked the woman from the catering table with the pink trucker hat. She was now sitting on the back of an open production truck and appeared only slightly more engaged than she had twenty minutes ago.

"DP's having an allergic reaction," the woman said. "He's got his EpiPen, though. Luckily."

"Allergic reaction?" Maya asked. "What did he—" Her voice trailed off, then she stopped and took a sharp breath in as her stomach sank and blood rushed to her cheeks. "Cam?" she asked weakly, the weight of her idiotic mistake landing like a brick.

"Yeah," said the woman. "Not sure what caused it, but his tongue started to swell, so they called emergency services right away."

Maya's mind raced as the image of Cam plucking a cookie off the plate, distracted and trusting, played in her mind.

"The cookies," she whispered, her eyes filling with tears. "They have almond flour in them."

"Those cookies had *almond flour* in them?" the woman said, narrowing her eyes and standing up. "This is a nut-free set!" If only Trucker Hat had been this alert earlier. "I'd better go inside and let them know," she said, disdain dripping from her voice.

"Tell them I'm so sorry," Maya said, a lump forming in her throat. She scooped up the plate and beelined it back to the bakery, tossed the other cookies immediately into the trash, then sat at the counter with her head in her hands.

How had she not thought of that? She had a disclaimer prominently displayed on her door and on the glass case to alert customers that all her products were likely exposed to nuts and gluten, a public precaution that made her less conscious of the ingredients she was using in her products. She had her bases covered as far as customers who came into the store—but still, how could she have made such an idiotic oversight?

She knew why. All she was thinking about, selfishly, was herself and getting back on set.

She stood by the door, wringing her hands together, and watched as Cam followed the paramedics out to the ambulance. She was slightly relieved to see that before he jumped into the back of the van, he turned around to give the crew, who had gathered around, a thumbs-up as they waved and clapped for him.

Maya breathed out slowly. He would be okay. But what a near disaster. What if he hadn't had his EpiPen on him? She might have been charged with manslaughter.

The ambulance made a three-point turn, and when it drove by the bakery, Maya almost hid her face in shame.

Her flight instinct kicked in again when she saw Will striding down the street from the set, right in the direction of the bakery. There was no time to lock the doors and kill the lights.

Will flung the door open and stood in the entrance to the bakery, gaping at her. "What the hell, Maya? You're trying to kill my crew?"

Maya felt the tears welling up again. "I didn't mean to—"

"Thank goodness he's going to be fine," Will said. He let out a huff. "You said almond flour, right?" The room was silent. Maya didn't know what to say. Will shook his head. "Thank goodness he only has a light allergy to almonds."

"Oh, thank goodness," Maya said, but she couldn't summon any other words to make it better.

"And now we've lost an entire half a shoot day," Will

said, his eyes flashing. "Honestly, Maya." He ran his hands through his hair and looked away from her.

"If there's anything I can do, I just—"

Will sighed. "I know you didn't mean any harm. Just—"

"Just stay away," Maya said. "I get it."

Silence hung in the air. "All right. I'd better get to the hospital and check on Cam," Will said.

"Let me know if there are any updates," she called as he disappeared back onto Main Street and left her standing behind the counter, feeling very foolish and, once again, very small.

Chapter Ten

"Glad you're okay, man," Will said as they pulled into the Briarwood's lot. He'd stuck with Cam while the hospital monitored him for a couple of hours and declared him safe to go. "You didn't panic at all."

"This happens more than you think," Cam said. Will locked the car and together they scaled the steps to the inn. "It's partially my fault. I should have asked what was in them."

"But we promised you a nut-free set, so," Will said.

A FaceTime call came in from Cam's girlfriend, so Will excused himself to his room, where he took a hot shower and sent some texts about the next day. They were going to extend the shoot day by two hours, which meant paying overtime and creeping ever closer to the limit of their budget. On day three, this wasn't a good place to be.

What could have possibly compelled Maya to bring an allergen bomb to set like that? She'd been right there at the restaurant when Cam pulled out his EpiPen.

But even then, he thought about the fear and remorse in Maya's eyes when he'd entered the bakery. Had he been too hard on her?

He toweled off and shook his head, threw on a new

pair of jeans and a T-shirt, flopped back in his bed and picked up his phone.

Cam's okay, he typed. Sorry if I overreacted. Any of those cookies left?

A moment later, his text was marked as read. He watched as it looked like a message was coming through, then the typing on the other end stopped.

Will knew Maya felt badly. He didn't want her worrying about it all night.

He waited five minutes, then sent another message. Looking forward to seeing your star turn tomorrow, he typed again. I promise minimal notes.

He waited again, and ten seconds later, a single smile emoji, followed by a star, appeared on his screen. He grinned and tossed the phone on his bed, then shook his head again.

He dug into his overnight bag and pulled out the paperback version of Maya's book, the one he'd bought after signing the contract.

Now that the shoot day was cut short, he'd heard something about a book club happening downstairs tonight. He'd never been part of a book club, but he liked books, and he liked clubs. Why not tonight?

Maya checked her lipstick in the mirror and took a deep breath. She'd contemplated canceling, but it was too last minute. She just hoped she didn't run into Cam and that Will was busy getting ready for the next day.

Butterflies fluttered in her stomach. The next day. There was no reason to be worried about the shoot—she didn't even have to deliver any lines, just hand over some cookies and smile, which was a central component of her job that she had lots of practice with.

When Will's texts had come through, she'd half expected he was telling her they were replacing her the next day and they had a restraining order out for the health and safety of the cast and crew.

Instead he'd been…sweet?

No. He was just putting her at ease, which was fair. Obviously she'd be worried about Cam. Will had his annoying tendencies, but at the end of the day, he wasn't a complete jerk. Letting her know that there wasn't a major health catastrophe was just the courteous thing to do.

However, it wasn't at all helpful in her quest to dim the light on this new attraction she was feeling for Will, not just physically—although, ugh, that was strong—but she had to admit that she liked who he'd matured into. If it weren't for this creative tug-of-war she found herself in, it was hard to deny that she might actually enjoy spending time with him.

Tomorrow, she'd be under the lights, his eyes on her. It was…unnerving.

That was a worry for later. Tonight, she had to be at her best for a roomful of ladies who had not only generously purchased her book but had taken the time to read it and spend their night talking about it.

When Maya entered the front foyer at the Briarwood Inn, she was greeted by a light scent of freesia from the bouquet on the check-in desk and the sound of easy soul music wafting in from the front room. The decor of the space was warm but modern, with paintings by local artists adorning the walls, gleaming hardwood floor with a silk runner welcoming guests into the space, and a chandelier casting warm light over the entrance.

The book club was scheduled to begin at seven, but she figured she'd show up a few minutes early and maybe get a chance to meet Noah and Grace's little one.

Balancing the box of Portuguese custard tarts she'd made especially for the occasion, she peeked around the corner and found three women already sitting with her book on their laps, holding glasses of wine and nibbling on the hors d'oeuvres set up on the table in the middle of the circle. The sight of Mrs. Anderson's face lighting up when she spotted Maya almost made her miss the man sitting with his back to the entrance—cross-legged, baseball cap on and, from the angle, what looked like a knowing smile on his face.

"Maya!" Mrs. Anderson said. "So happy you could join us!"

Will turned at the sound of her name, and Maya noticed the copy of her book in his hand. It looked well-worn, with small colorful Post-its sticking out from the pages. Not only had Will read her book, but he'd actually *studied* it?

"Hey, Maya," Will said. "Hope you don't mind if I join. When Grace told me the book club was meeting here tonight and that they were reading my favorite new book—"

"We just thought, how perfect! The writer and director. When will we ever have another chance like this?" Sitting right beside Mrs. Anderson was Mrs. Campbell, clutching her copy of the book, beaming. Maya sensed it wasn't the time to veto the invitation.

"Chance of a lifetime," Maya managed, just as Grace

poked her head around the corner from the inn's kitchen with a baby carrier strapped to her body.

"Hey, Maya," she said, smiling. She carried two bottles of wine to the table and set them down.

"You know we're fine with our boxed wine, Grace," Mrs. Anderson said.

"Speak for yourself," said Allison Yip, the retired nurse and main book club organizer. She picked up the bottle and surveyed the label. "This looks nice. Thanks, Grace."

"And who's this little one?" Maya cooed.

Grace approached and angled herself so Maya could see the six-month-old baby fast asleep against her mother's chest. "My assistant," she said, smiling.

"She's beautiful," said Maya. She was still very much on the fence of whether she wanted children of her own someday, but she loved the velvety smooth skin, the teeny tiny noses and soft wispy hair.

When she glanced up, she found Will looking at her with a mixture of curiosity and skepticism. "Anything cute, pretty, sparkly or shiny," he said to the women in the circle, "Maya is there for it."

"Just because I don't gravitate to dark, serious, boring and—and—" She struggled to find a word. "Stupid," she said.

"Stupid?" said Will, cocking an eyebrow.

Maya felt her cheeks flush. He'd always been so good at diminishing the things she liked and spent time thinking about. And now here he was, not only invading her town, but for goodness sake's, the freaking book club?

"You're really going to stay?" she asked quietly, a smile on her face but a screw-you tone in her voice.

"Of course I am," said Will. "What kind of guest would I be, turning down an invite when I'm staying just one flight of stairs from here?"

"One who understood boundaries," Maya said, her smile unwavering.

"Hello, everyone!" called a voice from behind her, and she turned to find two more book-toting club members.

Maya took in a steadying breath, then sat in the chair directly across the circle from Will. She was avoiding eye contact but could just feel him looking at her smugly. This might be fun for him. But she took the book club seriously. The fact that a group of people would not only spend money on her work but would take the time to get together to discuss it? She'd only ever done two other book clubs, one in Barrie and one in Toronto, but both times, she'd dressed up and stayed later than requested, signed and personalized every book and taken selfies.

So he could sit there and smirk and make some kind of esoteric remark that only she knew was minimizing her writing. But she would be a pro and make sure all the book club ladies left eager to buy her next book.

"All right, everyone, let's get started," Allison said. "We have a very special guest with us this evening—two special guests, in fact—so let's give a big warm welcome to Maya Monroe and Will Hastings!"

Maya couldn't help but start at the sound of their names together again. Maya and Will. Will Hastings and Maya Monroe. Monroe and Hastings. For so long they'd been a pair, a duo, joined at the hip and voted the yearbook's 'most in-love couple.' She took a quick, steadying breath, then plastered her most confident and convincing grin on her face.

"Thank you for having me," she said, then glanced up at Will. "Us, I guess."

"I'm just here to talk about the book," said Will. "Thanks for the invite."

Maya shifted in her seat.

"I have a question I'd like to ask," said Allison.

"Ask away," said Maya.

Allison flipped through the pages until about the third-way mark. "The part of the story where Sarah and Ben go to the Christmas tree farm and get caught in his truck during an unexpected snowstorm. I just loved that part!"

Maya felt her cheeks go an unnatural shade of red. She couldn't bring herself to look at Will. The truth was, that very same moment had happened to them early in their relationship, and she'd thought about it while writing it. Back when she never expected this story to ever see the light of day, never mind make its way into Will's hands.

"I have to agree with Allison," Will piped up. "It reads as so…realistic."

She shot a look at him across the table. "Thank you," she said, smiling through gritted teeth. "Next question?"

She operated on autopilot for the next thirty minutes, trying to be gracious in accepting compliments and answering questions in a way that she hoped gave the book club ladies enough of a peek behind the curtain.

She bid the club members each farewell, and just as she was about to put on her jacket and get home for bed—at nine thirty, it was already her bedtime—Will approached and extended his copy of the paperback.

"Can I bother you to sign this for me?" he said. His gray T-shirt clung to his solid frame with annoying perfection, and she noted that he must have shaved before book club. His skin was smooth and soft-looking over the sharp line of his jaw, begging to be touched.

"I know you're making fun of me," said Maya.

Will gave her a look of mock indignation. "I don't know what would give you that idea. I'm here, at your book club, with a marked-up copy of your book. Which, I might remind you, I'm bringing to life in spectacular fashion for millions of people to see. It might just sell you a few more copies."

Maya fought the urge to roll her eyes. "Oh, so I'm supposed to get down on my knees and worship you now?"

Will's eyes sparkled with mischief. "I mean... I wouldn't be opposed to it."

She wanted to punch him. She wanted to kiss him. Instead, she plucked the book from his hands. "Fine. I'll sign your book," she said and removed her pen from her purse again.

She thought for a second, then scrawled a message and her signature on the inside title page, then plopped it back into his waiting hands and gave herself a mental pat on the back for her quick thinking.

He took the book from her. "This is worth even more now," he said. "Thank you." He flipped it open and read the inscription out loud. "May the spirit of Christmas wash away your skepticism and indifference to the magic of love." He looked up and started to laugh. "Wow."

"I have to go," said Maya.

"Actually," Will said, flipping the book shut, "would you have a second to look over something for me?"

"What is it?" said Maya. "I should really get home to bed. Life of a baker, you know."

"It's upstairs. Come have a look?"

Upstairs? To his room? Her stomach fluttered. How would that look if one of the other crew members happened to see her exiting the director's suite?

"I'll keep the door open. Relax," Will said.

"I am relaxed."

"The way you're clutching your purse tells me otherwise." Will's gaze shifted to her clenched fist, which was indeed holding onto her purse for dear life, as though it held her good sense and was about to be snatched right out of her hands.

Maya forced herself to loosen her grip and did her best to smooth her expression. Of course Will always noticed the little details. He dealt in the subtleties of human behavior. She wasn't going to give away more than she already had. "Well, what is it?" she said, with what she hoped was a nonchalant shrug. "I have ten minutes."

"Follow me."

Will led her up the wide staircase to the second floor of the Briarwood, her boots barely making a sound on the polished wood. She'd never been to the area where the inn's suites were, but she'd heard great things from the guests who visited the bakery now and then: the views. The refined decor. The serenity. It felt like the perfect place for a romantic getaway weekend, the polar opposite of what she was there for.

When Will opened the door, her sense was confirmed. The room was spacious and overlooked the lake, with what was surely a spectacular view when it wasn't dark outside. Cozy flames flickered in the gas fireplace on the far wall, which had two reading chairs in front of it. Through the bathroom door, she spotted a deep tub, perfect for a long relaxing soak, and the comforter on the king-size bed looked like it might swallow someone whole, in the most inviting way possible.

"Nice," she said. "Not a bad place to stay for a couple of weeks."

"I thought about staying with my dad—"

"And you figured you'd better survive your time here instead."

"Exactly," said Will, a faint smile on his lips but with that same flicker of resignation whenever the topic of his father came up. Maya and Gene had always gotten along well—she knew very well he found her charming—but the tension in Will and his father's relationship had always been an unspoken presence in the background of their time together. "And it's working out fine."

Maya couldn't help the flicker of sympathy she felt for him. It was sad, actually, that after all this time, he and his father hadn't resolved their issues. It wasn't that their relationship was terrible, in the way that some tumultuous parent/child relationships could be. But as much as she hated to admit it, Will was at his heart a good person, and so was Gene—it felt like a shame that they hadn't sorted things out and figured out a way to be a positive presence in one another's lives.

But she knew Will, and he wouldn't want to talk about it. Not that she in any way felt like opening the door to that kind of intimacy, especially in what felt like an uber intimate setting.

"I found this at my dad's, actually," he said, picking up a blue Adidas shoebox from the bedside table.

"Hopefully your feet haven't grown."

"I see your wonderful sense of humor hasn't changed."

Maya couldn't help but indulge the small smile that tugged at the edge of her lips. "All right, what did you want to show me?"

Will flipped up the box lid, pulled out a stack of photos and passed them to her.

Maya surveyed the first one in the pile, of her and Will at the picnic table in front of the school. She remembered that day vividly. They'd just finished their English exam and were studying for the math exam the next day. Will was showing her how to find the rate of change of a function, and she was annoyed by how easily it came to him but grateful for the help at the same time.

"Look how young we look," she murmured. She looked up at him. "And why you ever got rid of the undercut is beyond me."

"I'm thinking of bringing it back," he said, grinning. "Wait until you see the next one."

She flipped to the next picture, which made her laugh out loud. She was dressed as Dorothy from *The Wizard of Oz*, red sparkly heels and all, while Will was sporting the Tin Man costume Maya had made for him out of cardboard, aluminum foil, silver spray and duct tape. "You would only agree to a couple's costume if it had something to do with a classic film."

Will chuckled. "I still can't believe we didn't win the prize that year."

"We definitely got robbed," Maya agreed.

She shuffled through the rest of the photos, some of the two of them, some in their larger group of friends. "We had fun, didn't we?" she said, the irritation of his presence at book club now dulled.

"We sure did," said Will. "Lots of good memories."

She let his words hang in the air, fighting the urge to remind him that he'd ruined it, but ruining this moment didn't feel like the right thing to do.

Instead, she tucked the photos back into the shoebox and passed it back to him. "Thanks for showing me those," she said. "I should go."

Will nodded. "I enjoyed that, tonight," he said. "People seem to really love your writing."

The compliment melted over her. She didn't want it to mean as much as it did. "Thanks for coming," she said, pausing in the room's doorway. Part of her wanted to stay and ask what else was in the shoebox. What other items had he tucked away in there, assigned value to? Birthday cards she'd given him? The notes she'd passed him between classes, folded up into little origami birds? The postcard she'd sent to his dorm in Los Angeles, the day after he'd left town and the day before she'd gotten his text? It had mortified her, knowing that it would still take a couple of weeks before it arrived, and by then, he'd have all but forgotten about her.

The memory made her take another step away. They'd had their fun, once upon a time. But their story wasn't one with a happy ending, and the fact that he was leaving town again in a couple of weeks confirmed that. "Good night, Will," she said.

"Night, Maya," said Will.

She moved through the doorway into the hall and closed the door behind her. She stood there for a moment, taking a deep breath, then descended the steps and let herself out the Briarwood's front entrance into the dark cool air of the parking lot, very much past her bedtime but very much no longer tired.

Chapter Eleven

"Your skin is incredible," murmured Halle, dabbing a light coating of foundation over Maya's forehead.

"Thanks," Maya said to the makeup artist, grinning at her reflection in the mirror. "I've been drinking extra water all week for this."

"Just a little lipstick, and you're all set."

Shauna popped her head around the corner and pushed her headset away from her face. "All set?" she asked. "You look great!"

Halle stood back to inspect Maya and added one last swipe of her lipstick brush. "She's ready. Break a leg, Maya!"

Maya followed Shauna out of the makeshift hair and makeup area at the back of the production office, down Main Street and back to Flour Child.

There was barely any room inside the bakery to maneuver around the lights and equipment. Maya was pleased to see the set department had kept most of her decor intact and had layered Christmas decorations over every available space. The bakery case was filled with treats covered in red, white and green sprinkles and icing.

Maya stepped behind the counter and allowed the wardrobe supervisor to tie an apron over her emerald green button-down shirt. "Let me fix that for you," the woman said as Halle reached over and fussed with Maya's hair.

The door to the bakery opened, and Will entered, wearing a black hoodie and holding a coffee and his clipboard. He found her immediately, his eyes flashing with admiration. "Look at you," he said, a teasing smile playing on his lips. "I'd have mistaken you for a real baker."

Maya grinned. "Glad I'm passing for the real deal."

Will raised an eyebrow. "You all set?"

"Let's do this."

Maya stood behind the counter waiting for direction as Ginger and Blake entered the bakery wearing full winter attire. She was glad to be in just a button-down shirt. Between the warmth of the lights and the way being close to Will had her pulse racing, any other layer would have her sweating through Halle's carefully applied makeup.

"Just a tad to the left," said Skylar from behind the monitor. "And take a small step back."

Stu handed her a white cardboard box. "You'll put the cookies in here," he said. "Then hand them to Ginger."

Maya gave a nod, already feeling in her element. "I think I can handle that," she said.

"Don't forget to smile," said Will.

She locked eyes with him, and despite the bright light blinding her, there was no mistaking the look of approval in his eyes. She'd wondered if it would bother her, taking direction from him. But she liked it. A lot.

"Quiet on set," called Skylar. "And we're rolling."

Maya watched as Skylar counted down two, then one. She didn't need to force the smile on her face as Ginger and Blake approached the counter.

"Two of the gingerbread cookies," said Blake.

Maya took the cardboard box, slid the two cookies in and passed them to Blake. She even remembered to smile.

"And cut," Will called. "That was perfect."

"That was it?" said Maya.

"You nailed it," Ginger said, winking. "A total natural."

It was fun being under the lights. Having Will focused on her so intently. She hadn't expected it, but she didn't want it to end.

"Wait," she said. "Is it weird they don't pay for the cookies?"

Will shrugged. "It's going to be in a montage."

"I think we should do it again," Maya said. She half expected Will to tell her to roll his eyes and tell her not to interfere, but instead, he paused, locking eyes with her, the shift in the air around them leaving her almost breathless.

"Let's set up," Will said.

Maya noticed Blake and Ginger exchange a look, but everyone else moved to their places. The set decorator returned the cookies to the display case while a gaffer fiddled with a light.

While she waited, Maya looked back up at Will. A small smile played on the corner of his lips. She knew she was being indulged. And she liked it.

They rolled again, this time with Blake passing a five-dollar bill across the counter.

"Okay that it's Canadian money?" Maya asked.

Will raised an eyebrow. "It's set in Canada, so I think it's okay. Is someone trying to get another take?"

He joined Maya behind the counter as Blake and Ginger disappeared out the front and the rest of the crew started to strike the set.

"I still can't believe all of that, for ten seconds," Maya said.

"The magic of cinema," Will said. He took a seat on the stool next to her, close enough that they could talk without everyone hearing them. "But really, you looked amazing on screen."

The compliment lit her up inside. "Can I see?" said Maya.

"Not until release day," Will said, his eyes twinkling. He was flirting with her.

"Unfair," Maya said.

"They're going to strike the set now," said Will. "Want to grab a coffee?"

She very much wanted to. "I'd better stick around here and clean up," Maya said. "I want to open for the afternoon."

"I thought you said something about inviting your parents out for the shoot," Will asked. "Did they change their minds?"

"I thought about it," Maya said. "But my dad…" She stopped and laughed. "I don't want to put you in harm's way. He was pretty ticked off when you broke up with me like that, and he had to deal with a heartbroken daughter."

"Fair enough," said Will. "If it were my daughter, I think I'd be pretty ticked off, too."

It was the closest he'd ever come to apologizing, and hearing him say the words felt good.

It didn't take long before the bakery was emptied of all the equipment and Maya was setting out a light offering of a few types of bread to sell along with the pastries she'd made the day before. Just enough to get her to the end of the day.

She watched through the front window as the flurry of activity continued outside.

Her star moment had been short-lived, but it had been a great morning. She found herself unable to stop thinking about the look in Will's eyes after he called cut. The way he'd nodded at her, his gaze full of something she couldn't quite name. It wasn't just approval—it was something warmer, more intimate. It made her heart flutter, and in that quiet moment, she knew she wouldn't soon forget it.

Fifteen minutes before closing, just as she was starting the final tasks in her cleanup, the door to the bakery opened.

Lucas passed through, with a mop of sandy blond hair in his face and a drawn expression. He wore a Buffalo Bills hoodie and a pair of jeans and, like most teenagers she saw in town, had his phone plastered to his hand and AirPods in his ears. His eyes were a piercing blue, and he had full lips and a muscular frame. He was a nice-looking kid, like a member of a boy band, of which he'd be the token bad boy.

"Hey, Lucas," Maya said. "I was hoping you'd drop by."

Lucas tapped the screen of his phone and removed one ear bud. "Sorry. I didn't hear you."

"I just said that I was hoping you'd be by this week. Your mom mentioned you were still looking for a job."

"*She's* still looking for a job. For me."

Maya resisted the urge to raise an eyebrow and tell

Lucas that his mom was only trying to do the best for him, and the best thing for any teenager was to have a part-time job, but she sensed that she'd catch more flies with honey with this kid.

"Well, you came at a good time," Maya said. "Today's laundry day. I have a bunch of tea towels and cloths that need cleaning that I really don't feel like lugging home. If you take them down the street to the laundromat, then fold them and bring them back, I'll pay you twenty-five bucks. You can literally sit in the laundromat and look at your phone the whole time."

"Twenty-five dollars?" Lucas said dubiously.

"Tax free," said Maya. "That would be for today only, though. You don't have to commit to anything. But if you like the feeling of that extra money in your pocket, there's more where that came from."

"I'll do the towels," Lucas said. "But my mom said the job starts before the sun comes up. That's…not really my thing."

Maya grinned. "You get used to it. And another bonus," she said, plucking a shortbread from the case and passing it to him, "is the taste-testing quality control component of the job."

Lucas looked at the cookie suspiciously, as though there was a chance it might explode in his hand.

"Try it," she urged.

Lucas took a bite, but his expression remained unchanged.

"Well?" said Maya.

"Pretty good," Lucas muttered, wiping the crumbs from his face.

Maya picked up the laundry bin full of towels. "You're

welcome," she said. "If I'm not here when you get back, I'll be on the street watching the filming. You can find me there."

Lucas rolled his eyes. "I heard they're filming some kind of dumb romance movie. My mom loves that stuff."

Maya resisted the urge to say something snarky. "What's wrong with a little happily-ever-after?" she said.

"It's just…so unrealistic," Lucas said.

"Aspirational," Maya corrected him. She opened the till and extracted some change for the laundromat. "Here," she said. "I'll see you in an hour and a half. Text your mom and tell her where you are, all right?"

"All right," mumbled Lucas. "Twenty-five bucks, you said?"

"And whatever you want from the display case, if you fold everything nicely," said Maya.

Lucas picked up the laundry sack and disappeared through the front door.

Maya glanced at her watch. Usually, the next two hours of a Thursday evening would be reserved for a quick dinner and then she'd be at her laptop, drafting a new chapter.

But tonight, she had other plans.

The big floodlights were brighter now that the sun was starting to disappear behind the tree line. It had cooled off a bit. The actors were probably happy now to be clothed in winter gear.

Maya approached where the small group of Sunset County residents was gathered, watching from afar as the Christmas tree-decorating scene appeared to be well underway.

"Can you hang that one with your left hand this time?" Skylar called from the monitor where she stood beside Will.

"All right," Ginger responded, and moved the small puppy dog ornament to her other mitten-covered hand. "Right here good?"

"All good," called Will. "Quiet on set. We're rolling. And three, two."

Ginger and Blake waited a beat. "There's no way this tree isn't going to win," Blake said.

Ginger grinned a one-thousand-watt smile. "If you say so," she said.

Maya remembered reading this part of the script, where they'd kept the dialogue mostly the same as the book. She mouthed along the next line with Ginger. "Although I think a good chunk of the population of Garrison Creek are cat people."

Ginger nailed the line, but just as she was about to place the ornament on the tree, Will's voice cut through the air. "Cut there," he said.

Maya bristled. What fault could he find in that?

She watched as Will huddled with Shauna, then walked over to the actors. "All right, listen," he said, "Let's change that line to 'I think half of Garrison Creek is allergic to dogs.'"

What? Maya blinked, dumbfounded. What a ridiculous change. Did he even realize that many romance readers were obsessed with cats? That line had been a playful nod to them, a little in-joke.

Her hands clenched. It took everything in her not to step through the stanchion and march right up to him again. She could already picture his face if she did—annoyed, defensive, ready to shut her down.

No, that wouldn't go over well. She'd promised to play nice.

Instead, she drifted closer to the monitor area, hoping Will would notice her. Maybe if he did, he'd think twice before messing with a line that had taken hours to get right.

She watched the next take, and the line sounded even dumber coming out of Blake's mouth than it had from Will's.

"Got it," Will said. "Great job. Let's move on to the judging."

"We need the mayor and assistant," Shauna said in her mic. "Take five, everyone."

A cool breeze fluttered down Main Street. Maya tucked her chin into the collar of her coat just as Will's gaze shifted over.

He left his post at the monitor and moved to where she was standing. "I know you're not happy with the dialogue change," he said.

"I don't know what you're talking about," said Maya.

Will raised an eyebrow. "It's okay. I probably won't use it. It's just that sometimes it's nice to have options. Thank you for not making a fuss about it."

Maya nodded, relief washing over her.

"Everything looks great, huh?" Will said, gesturing to the fifteen-foot fir trees, festooned with lights and garlands, all the ornaments specific to the trees' themes.

It did look great. It was pure Christmas magic. Maya wanted to give him hell for the line change, but the way his face lit up, like he was actually enjoying directing her movie—she softened a little. "What's the snow made from?" she asked.

"It's a mix of shredded Styrofoam, cotton and faux snow spray," Will said. "Lightweight, easy to work with.

We'll have some falling during the Christmas tree farm scene. Which—" He paused, his deep eyes searching hers, "I'm scouting this weekend. They gave me a couple of options. I'm going to check them out on Saturday. If you want to join."

The correct answer was no. Not only did Maya have to finish chapters eight and nine on her work in progress after closing the bakery, if she had any hope of meeting her next deadline, but the idea of spending more time with Will, getting wrapped up in the fantasy of him... No matter how tempting it was, it wasn't just a terrible idea. It was a minefield.

She searched for the words to say no but couldn't find them. The truth was, she did want to go. She wanted to jump in the front seat of Will's rental car and take full control of the stereo the way she used to. She wanted to put her hand over top of his on the gearshift and crack jokes and implore him to slow down on the bends of the county roads and pull over on a quiet cottage lane, a place owned by city people who weren't in town, and make out in the back seat until past curfew.

Except this time, they weren't teenagers, and they could do whatever they wanted, whenever they wanted.

What did she want with Will? His now broader shoulders, wiser eyes. His experience with other women, not that she wanted to think too much about that. She badly wanted to be alone with Will, away from the spotlights and gaffers and set pieces and all of Sunset County watching.

"Mayor and assistant walking," a voice called over the walkie.

Will pulled the device off the belt of his jeans. "Got

it," he said, then looked at her. "Ten o'clock Saturday," he said. "Meet me at Rise and Grind if you want to come."

"I'm at the bakery Saturday," she barely eked out. "But thanks."

She thought she detected a hint of disappointment in his eyes, but he just gave her his adorable half smile, then turned and walked back to the monitor where Cam was waiting for him.

Out of the corner of her eye, she saw Lucas making his way down the sidewalk with the stack of folded towels in his arms. She waved, then joined him at the entrance of the bakery. "Nice job," she said, nodding to the stacks. "Listen, if I happened to need someone to cover the cash for a couple of hours on Saturday, would you happen to be free?"

"Wait, so do I like…have the job or something?"

"Let's call Saturday a trial. Come in tomorrow after school, and I'll train you on using the cash register and show you around. Sound good?"

"All right," said Lucas. He followed her into the bakery and passed her the basket of towels.

"Wait here," said Maya. She went behind the counter, opened the cash register and pulled out a twenty and a five-dollar bill, then passed them to Lucas. "And something to take to go?" she asked.

Lucas scanned the display case. "I guess those shortbreads were pretty good," he said.

Maya resisted the urge to laugh and instead slid two cookies into the paper sleeve. "One's for your mom, okay?"

"Thanks," Lucas said.

"See you tomorrow?" said Maya.

Lucas paused, as though he was making a commitment he might regret, then looked at the folded-up bills in his hand and shoved them into the pocket of his jeans. "See you tomorrow," he said.

Perfect, Maya thought. She wasn't going to join Will on Saturday. No way, no how. But his words echoed in her mind: *Sometimes it's nice to have options.*

Chapter Twelve

At five minutes after three o'clock on Friday, Maya was pretty sure that Lucas wasn't coming and that while he'd been happy to accept the twenty-five dollars and shortbread cookies, he'd come to his senses about the idea of getting up at the crack of dawn every day before school.

Maya couldn't blame him. Her favorite thing as a teenager was to sleep past noon on Saturdays, roll out of bed and grab the box of Lucky Charms from the cupboard and snack from it like a bag of chips in front of the TV while watching whatever was on the Disney channel until her mother shooed her out the door to get some fresh air. Did 4:00 a.m. even exist when she was a teenager?

A couple of customers came in, one to pick up the birthday cake they'd ordered for a celebration that evening, and another a loaf of French bread for dinner.

"Enjoy," said Maya. She pressed the receipt on the metal stake, and when she looked up, she was surprised to see Lucas passing through the door. His sandy blond hair dangled in his eyes, a light perspiration on his face.

"Sorry," he said. "I had detention after school. I came as fast as I could."

She was dying to ask what kind of behavior resulted in detention these days—online gambling during class?

Vaping in the bathroom? But she knew enough to understand that Lucas probably needed a few people in his life who didn't fully associate him with being a total screwup.

"You can throw your backpack behind the counter," Maya said. "Let me give you the tour."

She smiled to herself when she saw Lucas slide his phone out of his backpack before putting it away, then pause and slide it back in. Cassie must have had a talk with him about acceptable workplace behavior.

"All right," she said. "It's not a big place, so it won't take long, but there are a few really important safety considerations with the stoves and ovens and everything."

"Will I be…using those?" Lucas said.

Maya grinned. "Not yet, but happy to teach you at some point," she said. "I will, however, teach you how to use the bread slicer. It's got a safety latch, so it's pretty foolproof."

Lucas's shoulders relaxed. "All right," he said. He was a handsome kid. But a sparkling conversationalist he was not.

"Convection ovens are over here," Maya said, pointing to the back wall. "This larger chest is the fridge." She swung open the door. "Mostly dairy. You're not lactose intolerant, are you? That's a condition of employment."

"Ah, no," said Lucas. "I don't think so at least."

"Just a joke," said Maya. "Although butter is kind of a big deal around here. Basically, I need help for an hour in the morning cleaning up before we open and then boxing orders and doing some local delivery. You have a car, right?"

Lucas looked confused again. "I didn't know—"

"Kidding again. But we supply a couple of restaurants on Main Street with their bread, and twice a week Rise and Grind gets an order of our biscotti. They tried to make their own, but…" she winked "…they've accepted that mine are better. So you'll just need to make those deliveries by foot while I serve the first few customers."

"People actually come here for seven o'clock opening?" His voice was skeptical, but there was a hint of curiosity in his voice.

"Every day," she said. "And they get very cranky when I open even a minute late. So, having someone do the deliveries is key."

He raised an eyebrow but didn't probe any further.

She spent the next twenty minutes showing Lucas how to use the point-of-sale app on the iPad, then give him a rundown on her products and the main ingredients in each, in case a customer asked. "But if you forget, there's a binder here with everything listed."

"I have a good memory," said Lucas. He looked at her with a guarded expression, but there was a hint of pride in his voice.

"You must be a good science student then," Maya said. "I was terrible at bio. Too many terms to memorize."

"I'm not really a good anything student," Lucas said, shrugging. He shifted his weight. "I'm sure my mom has told you."

"Is that from ability or effort?" Maya said.

"Not sure," Lucas said. "Probably a bit of both."

Maya softened. "Well, around here, the most important thing is to be friendly to the customers. Smile. Make some polite small talk but not too much. People like to chat but also get on with their day."

"So many rules," said Lucas.

"People appreciate customer service. My products are great. But the service makes them better."

Lucas was quiet for a moment, his expression unreadable, but then he gave her a half nod, like he was actually *thinking* about what she said. "I'll keep that in mind."

"Why don't you tidy up the display case?" Maya said. "Grab that towel there. Take out the trays and wipe any crumbs, then move all the pastries to the front so everything looks full."

"And people still come in at this time of day?" Lucas said.

Just then, the bells above the entrance tingled, and a man with two small kids entered.

Maya smiled. "The after-school and work crowd. Our second rush."

Maya served the customers and kept an eye on Lucas as he took the wet towel and cleaned out the case, then took a pair of tongs and shifted the desserts. He moved tentatively, but with care. Like a little kid playing Jenga or Operation.

"Looks good," Maya said. She glanced at her watch. "Usually I wait until the shop closes to make the dough for tomorrow's bread, so it has time to rise in the fridge overnight. But if you're okay watching the front and helping anyone who comes in, I can start it now and leave earlier. I've got a cake to bake for the morning, too." She made a mental note to text Andie Carter about the Snow White cake.

Lucas nodded. "Sure," he said, and paused. "What do you mean, rise overnight?"

It always struck Maya... Something so basic and

primordial, bread being a staple of every generation throughout history, and so few people knew how to make the simple item, which cost pennies to make and only required subtle tweaks to create infinite variations.

"Come watch," Maya said. "We'll hear if anyone comes in."

She was happy to give Lucas a part-time job, to keep him out of trouble for Cassie and give him a chance to earn some pocket money. But maybe, more important, she could teach him a little about life along the way.

Chapter Thirteen

Of course, on the one day he could sleep in, Will lay wide awake shortly after five in the morning on Saturday, the sky outside still inky gray with only a hint that the sun would soon begin its ascent over the water. A perfect time to catch up on lost sleep throughout the week. To rest and get his brain working at full capacity, to let his legs, aching from standing for twelve hours a day, get some sweet relief.

But here he was, alert and aware that in five short hours, there was a chance he'd be spending the day with Maya. Driving around Sunset County with her in the passenger seat of his car. The idea of it was surreal. He felt like a kid on Christmas morning, waiting for his parents to tap on the door and allow him out of his room to see what Santa brought.

It was silly. It was a fool's errand. It was…kind of *high school*.

He rolled over and sighed and tried to fall asleep. At six o'clock, he reluctantly got out of bed, took a long shower, then descended to the front room to find the inn silent and still. Right. Breakfast began at seven on weekends.

He shrugged on his jacket and emerged from the inn,

the sun now glowing behind the trees and illuminating the gravel path to the parking lot. The plan was to go to his dad's after the scout for dinner, but he supposed there was nothing wrong with an extra visit.

The winding county roads were empty, lined by the maple and oak trees whose leaves would soon lay flatly on the ground before being covered by snow in what could be a matter of weeks. Winter came sooner here than it did in Brooklyn; Will could vividly remember a couple of Halloweens, trick-or-treating in his parka and coming home with his pillowcase filled not only with candy but snow.

Will tapped the door quietly a couple of times, then stepped into the foyer.

The house was still. There was a chance he'd just have a coffee and watch the news quietly and be gone again before Gene woke up, but he'd leave a note to let his dad know he'd been there.

Agatha poked her head from the kitchen.

"You're here early," Will said, and it occurred to him he had no idea what time her days started.

"I could say the same for you," she said and smiled. "I thought you were coming for dinner, not breakfast."

"I woke up early, so I thought I'd come around to see if the old man's up."

"He usually sleeps until seven. Then he'll nap again in the afternoon. Can I get you a coffee?"

"I can get myself something," said Will, kicking off his shoes. "Thank you."

"Two different real estate agents stopped by yesterday," Agatha said. She folded the dish towel she was using and hung it over the stove handle. "Not with clients or anything but hoping to see the space."

Will poured himself a glass of water. "How did my dad react?" Not well, he guessed.

"He was asleep," said Agatha.

"Good," said Will. He cleared his throat. "Has he said anything about the move?"

Agatha shook her head. "I've reminded him a few times what's happening, but he's either forgetting—"

"Or pretending to forget," Will said.

She raised her eyebrows. "Exactly."

"And you know this place?" Will asked. "Pinecrest Haven?"

Agatha nodded. "He'll be in good hands. My niece manages the front desk, actually. I've given her strict orders to look out for your father."

"Appreciate it," said Will.

There was a rustling from down the hallway.

"That's him," said Agatha. "Feel free to come say good morning. Just know that he's usually a little disoriented when he wakes up."

Will followed Agatha to the bedroom and found Gene with his eyes half open, trying to get out of bed. He felt like an intruder for a moment, watching his father in such a vulnerable state, his normally well-combed hair askew, seeming unable to extricate himself from the sheets without Agatha's assistance.

"Good morning, Gene," she said cheerfully. "Sit up first, and you can put your feet in your slippers."

Gene grunted softly, then took hold of the forearm that Agatha extended to him. Slowly, he sat up, then allowed her to guide him from the bed to a standing position, where he paused for a minute, then noticed Will in the doorway.

It struck Will that without Agatha, Gene would likely be unable to get out of bed on his own. The deterioration was so clear and visible, and for a moment, Will experienced another wave of guilt for the amount of time he'd been away and how little he really knew about Gene's condition. When had it started getting this bad? And what would Gene have done without the money Will had sent to hire Agatha?

"Hey, Dad," Will said.

Gene shrugged on the robe that Agatha was helping him pull on. "Thought you weren't coming until dinner," he said. So he'd remembered. The unpredictability of how Gene's mind was at once working and stalling struck Will.

"I was up early, so thought I'd come by for coffee," Will said. "I'll let you get dressed. See you in the living room."

Will sat on the sofa, listening as Agatha cheerily assisted Gene through his morning routine. His phone buzzed in his pocket, and he slid it out to find a text from Maya.

Still planning on driving around today? it read.

He waited a minute before responding. Sure am, he typed. See you at the coffee shop?

A moment later, a thumbs-up appeared on the screen. Will smiled to himself and glanced out the window as the sun cleared the trees and the breeze rippled the water slightly. Regardless of how this conversation went, it was shaping up to be a good day.

* * *

The conversation, as it turned out, did not go very well at all. Will presented the plan, and Gene was having none of it.

"Dad," Will said, doing his best to maintain a calm tone of voice. "We agreed to this, remember? That's why I'm in town."

"Took you booting me out of my own goddamn home to get you back here," Gene said. "I'm not going anywhere."

"The level of care you're going to require soon," Will said, "is more than Agatha can take on. You need to be somewhere where help is always less than a minute away."

"You think you know what's best," Gene said. "You've always thought that way."

Will bristled. He wanted to bite back, but it wouldn't help. "The listing is going live on Monday," he said. "Thanksgiving Day. And a week from then, we've scheduled your move. The house will start to show, and no offers will be accepted without me passing them by you."

"What's the damn point in me signing off, anyway?" said Gene, shaking his head. "I'll be locked in that prison for the rest of my life. What the hell am I going to do with that money? You might as well go right ahead and cash the check right into your bank account. Save the inheritance tax when I kick the bucket."

Regardless of what was going on, the old man's brain was still sharp in some ways. Gene actually had a point. But it wasn't about the money. Will was doing more than fine on his own.

He glanced at his watch. He wanted to get back to the

inn and send a few emails before meeting Maya at the coffee shop, but he didn't want to leave on a bad note. "Hey, Dad. I uh, wanted to tell you about a new project I'm working on," he said. Gene was a big Herman Melville fan. This might even impress him.

Gene said nothing, so Will continued, "It's a biopic of Herman Melville. All about his life as a writer and time working in the whaling industry."

Gene grunted. "Back when real men worked real jobs," he said.

Will scoffed. "For goodness' sake, Dad," he said, and stood up. So much for leaving on good terms. "Forget it. I'll see you later on." Will shook his head, flicked on the news and passed Gene the remote before collecting his jacket and keys.

He'd tried.

Any last trace of Will's annoyance melted away when a couple hours later, he pulled up in front of Rise and Grind to find Maya sitting in the window with her laptop. She didn't see him at first, so he took a moment to watch as she bit the corner of her lip and tapped away at her keyboard, seemingly lost in a chapter of whatever it was she was working on at the moment.

For a moment he allowed himself a daydream of them together on a quiet morning in his condo, sunlight pouring through the windows, the rich aroma of coffee filling the air and a soft jazz record playing in the background. Maya would be at the breakfast bar, immersed in her novel, while he sat on the couch, working on his script. Every so often they'd interrupt one another to talk about an issue they were having with their plots or a character's motivation. They'd know enough about one another's projects to help each other out, and after a few hours of work, they'd both be content to flip their screens closed and walk out the door to a local diner or café for a bite to eat.

He knew that Maya thought her stories were on the fluffier side. But when it came down to it, not everything he worked on was breaking new ground in cinema, either. Even his most well-received films often followed a well-trodden path—the classic hero's journey, the timeless tale of the stranger who comes to town.

When Maya looked up from her screen and spotted him in the car, she smiled and waved. Will suddenly couldn't believe that in just over a couple of weeks' time, that smile was about to disappear from his life again.

She held up a finger indicating that she'd be just a second, then packed her things into her bag. He got out of the car to greet her on the sidewalk and opened the passenger door.

"Morning," he said. "Getting some work done?"

"Well, I felt a little guilty slacking while Lucas is holding down the fort at the bakery. I finished a cake for a birthday party at Magical Beans early this morning," she said, gesturing down the street to the storefront with the gilded book hanging above the entrance, "and I figured I'd come here and stay close at hand in case he needed help."

"And?"

"So far so good," she said, a hint of pride in her voice. "I know more than a few people think I'm crazy for hiring him. But honestly? He's a sweet kid. He just needs to mature a little, figure himself out."

"You always did see the best in people," Will said. He warmed at the thought of her passing the keys to the bakery to a teen boy, a gesture that probably gave him a rush of responsibility and pride.

"And most of them rise to the occasion." She smiled at him as she tossed her bag in the back seat, then slid into the front. "All right, let's scout!" she said. "This feels like a treasure hunt or something."

Will got into the driver seat. "Well, technically the real scout already happened before I came to town. A few crew members came up to shoot some B-roll that I could look at from home. I haven't seen these spots in person, so this is more of a…confirmation, I guess."

"So what you mean is that you can still unconfirm them, if they don't happen to be just right?"

He glanced over, finding her eyebrow raised in that familiar challenge. "Well, the final call comes down to me," Will said. "So I guess, yeah, I could, if it isn't just right."

Maya leaned back in her seat, satisfaction written on her face. "Excellent," she said, the spark in her voice unmistakable. "Let's do this."

Will shook his head as he started the engine but couldn't hide the smile tugging at his lips.

Chapter Fourteen

Maya breathed in lightly, taking in the fresh scent of Will's aftershave which filled the cabin of the car. His casual outfit—faded jeans, a bomber jacket, a ball cap and sunglasses—wasn't flashy, but it was effortlessly cool. Nothing about it screamed designer, yet everything fit him so perfectly, she found herself wondering if he had an eye for this kind of thing himself or if someone else had a hand in curating his wardrobe.

It wasn't that his style had drastically changed since high school; it was just that now, there was a certain polish to it—a kind of refined ease—that made him seem even more striking. The blend of sharp features, that subtle confidence and the way his clothes hung off him made the term *full package* seem almost inadequate.

"The ski hill is an hour out of town, so we won't go there," Will said, pulling something up on his phone. "Plus it's really our only option in the area. But up next, the lodge's exterior." Maya watched as he punched an address into the GPS. "Wait until you see where it's shooting."

She noted the hint of excitement in his voice. It was the first time she'd felt him exhibit what looked like true enthusiasm for the project.

Maya tried to guess where in the vicinity of the town there was a place that matched her vision for the ski lodge. The lodge was one of the central locations in the book, where the bride and groom were staying along with the wedding party. Ben was the owner and manager of the front desk, and so, the gatekeeper of much of the information and access Sarah needed to pull off the perfect wedding. In her mind's eye, Maya pictured rustic wood and stone, with twinkly white lights in the towering pines that surrounded the building. She couldn't wait to see what Caroline would do with it.

"The fancy area of the lake," Maya noted as Will took a left down the road that led to the area's most exclusive cottage row. Wealthy couples from the city had taken over and were building cottages that were more like mini mansions, with boathouses bigger than her own home. The cottages themselves weren't visible from the road, and only a few could be seen from the lake when the trees had leaves on them. Otherwise, Maya had no business on the water once the leaves came down and the water froze over, so she had no idea what was hidden in this line of properties.

"So believe it or not, John Greenwood's assistant actually called the production office to offer his place as a location," Will said.

"You're shooting at John Greenwood's place?" Maya said, incredulous. John Greenwood was the owner of one of North America's largest privately owned homebuilding companies, and he had caused quite the stir in Sunset County when he bought a huge piece of property on Shaughnessy Lake. He'd been by the bakery once with a date, but he mostly kept to the property when he was in town and had a staff who managed all of the usual tasks that would necessitate someone going into town.

"Just the exterior," Will said. "The interior shots are in studio the week after we wrap up here."

Maya nodded. Of course. The studio shots. When Will and the whole production team left town. She wondered if it would all feel like a strange dream.

The GPS on the screen stopped navigating as soon as Will signaled a turn down an unmarked lane. "I think this is it," he said. "The notes said to turn at the boulder."

The gravel path curved to the right, and there were a couple of turnoffs on their left, which would lead to the water.

"It says to take the eighth driveway," Will said, navigating the car slowly along the well-groomed path.

"Remember when he first built this place?" Maya said. "And everyone was freaking out about what a giant cottage was being built in Sunset County?"

"Well, he started a trend, it seems like," Will said as an imposing structure came into view down one of the lanes. "I can't believe all this development."

"I mean, I'm not going to complain," said Maya. "I send a ton of delivery orders out this way. And Andie Carter gets a lot of bookings at her party center from parents with deep pockets. Which means over-the-top cakes. My specialty."

"Speaking of over the top," Will said, as he pulled into the long winding lane leading up to the Greenwood "cottage," which was more like a mini mansion plopped right into the woods.

The structure was gleaming in the early evening light. The crushed stone winding path from the road to the building was lined with white limestone concrete fire pits, which Maya imagined blazing in the evening as a welcome to the guests approaching the many parties John was known to host.

Will brought the car to a stop in the driveway. Maya exited the car and took in the impressive expanse of the property, with a wide view of the lake in the distance. She let out a low whistle. "I guess you're used to pulling up to this kind of place," Maya said, adjusting the strap of her purse. "With all the lavish parties you go to and everything?"

Will chuckled. "You make it sound like I'm a regular on the party circuit," he said.

"You're not?" Maya asked.

"Well, I've been to a few, I guess. But they get old," Will said. "Unless you're there with the right person." His lips turned up in an irresistible grin. "Apparently no one's on site right now, but the assistant said we can look around outside."

Maya scaled the front steps and peered through the window next to the imposing front door, which looked as though it was built to support a five-hundred-pound wreath. She scanned the interior of the estate that was visible from the window.

It was just as spectacular as the exterior. The ultra-modernist building's floor-to-ceiling windows offered an unobstructed view of Shaughnessy Lake from each floor. The design incorporated the rustic wood-and-stone building materials that were common to the Sunset County area, creating a sense of hominess and belonging despite the more modern architecture.

"Apparently it has eight bedrooms, five wood-burning

fireplaces, a separate spa building with a Finnish steam room and not only a vast wine cellar but a *cheese* cellar as well," Will said, peering into the window on the other side of the door.

"Who could possibly exist without a cheese cellar?" said Maya. "I just want to see the kitchen and what kind of appliances they have. Probably a Wolf. Or maybe a Gaggenau."

"Who could possibly exist without a Gaggenau?" Will teased. He looked around at the trees swaying overhead and the impressive facade of the building. "So what do you think? A good stand-in for the Garrison Creek Lodge?"

Maya considered, then stepped back to look at the exterior again, trying to imagine it decked out by Caroline and her team for Christmas. She tried to picture the lodge's painted wood sign hanging over the doorway, but somehow, it didn't quite fit.

On one hand, she knew that Will was happy to be filming at this location and was hopeful she'd be pleased with it, too. But try as she might, she couldn't summon the enthusiasm she knew he was seeking. It was gorgeous. It belonged in *Architectural Digest* magazine. But it just felt...off.

"It's really nice," Maya said. She paused.

"But..." Will said.

"But it's almost too nice. It's supposed to be a small town. This looks like a place that only millionaires would be able to afford to stay."

"The couple getting married is really well off," said Will. "Wouldn't they want to stay somewhere nice?"

"Yeah, but part of the reason they're getting married

in the small town is that the bride grew up there, and it's really sentimental for her," Maya said.

"So you hate it," said Will. He wore a tight smile, but there was resignation in his eyes.

"I don't hate it," Maya said. She did her best to summon some enthusiasm. "Once it's covered in lights and all Christmasy, it's going to look great," she said, then surveyed his expression. "What? You wanted my honest opinion. And my honest opinion is that…it has potential." She wasn't telling the whole truth, and the skeptical expression on Will's face told her he didn't buy it.

"Maybe the next stop will be a little more up your alley. Shall we hit the Christmas tree farm next?" Will said.

"Let's do it."

Will glanced sideways at Maya as they drove toward Morton's Tree Farm, just fifteen minutes from the Greenwood estate. She was looking out the window, seemingly lost in a daydream.

He was disappointed she hadn't been enthusiastic about the location for the lodge. But regardless, it was nice having her along, and he was glad for the opportunity to make her feel more involved, even if what he was showing her wasn't one hundred percent lining up with the world of her story in her mind's eye.

And the truth was, he agreed with her. Only days earlier, when she'd protested some changes he was making to the script and on set, had he gotten his back up and shot her down just because he didn't like being challenged?

He needed to check himself, if that was the case. At

the end of the day, even though Maya wasn't experienced in the world of film, she was incredibly smart, had great intuition and, to be fair, knew her story better than anyone else. He didn't want to get her hopes up by telling her this, but he was going to look into another location. It would have to be done quickly, though—the scene was set to shoot at the end of the week.

"I have to say, this is one of my favorite scenes from the book," Maya said.

"Well, your book club readers seemed to love it. Any particular reason why it's your favorite, too?" Will asked. He remembered reading it for the first time and wondering if Maya had just written it in service of the story, purely from imagination, or if there might have been a bit of memory injected in there, too.

"Are you asking if this scene is about us?" she asked.

He could tell she was studying him, but he kept his eyes trained on the road. "Well, I wasn't going to put it that bluntly, but yes," he said.

"It's not," she said simply.

If you say so, he thought, smiling to himself as he pulled into the parking lot following the Morton's Tree Farm sign that faced the road.

The tree farm spanned about two acres, with rows of fir trees growing in neat lines in sections of different sizes, each either months or years away from lighting up someone's home at Christmastime.

"Now this smell I can get behind," Maya said, cracking the window, a cool, pine-laced breeze entering the car. Will parked next to the red barn, which they'd be outfitting as a pop-up hot chocolate bar. "Can you translate that into film somehow?"

A man in an army green work jacket exited the barn as they were getting out of the car. "Hey there," the man said. "Welcome. Will Hastings?"

"Nice to meet you," Will said. "And this is Maya."

"Looking forward to having you all here for the shoot," Rick said. "Feel free to have a look around. I'll be inside if you need anything."

"Appreciate it," said Will. He wondered if Rick remembered the two kids who'd been stranded on his property for a few hours years ago, when snow squalls moved through the area, making it impossible to see your hand if you held it right up to your face.

He stood alone again with Maya, who was surveying the property.

"Why didn't you just pick Sugar Maple Farm or somewhere closer to town?" Maya asked.

"I just thought…" He paused and looked at her. "There's something special about this place."

Maya's eyes flashed with something. Approval? Desire? She paused and scanned the fields. "It looks a lot different here without snow," she said.

"You know Caroline will take care of that," said Will.

"The whole thing? That sounds expensive."

"Just what's immediately in frame," Will said. "Otherwise, we'll fix it in post."

It was a familiar film expression, a convenient excuse for mistakes made in production. But as he looked at Maya, remembering the perfection of their first time here together, he couldn't help but wish he could rewind to the moment he'd made the idiotic decision to let her go so carelessly.

If only he could edit that part of his past, like a bad take, and fix it in postproduction.

It had been the winter of their senior year. Will and Maya had taken Gene's truck into town to pick out a Christmas tree for Will's place, but the grocery store was sold out and the only ones left at the hardware store were sparse or crooked.

"Morton's Tree Farm," the shop attendant had offered. "I've heard a couple people say they've got great stock. It's about thirty minutes outside of town, but I think you'll find something there."

They'd made the drive through what started out as flurries. By the time they reached the tree farm, the snow was coming down so heavily, blowing through strong gusts of wind, that they'd had to sit in the truck in the parking lot for two hours waiting until it was safe to drive again.

"Since we're stuck here for a while," Will said. "Do you want your Christmas present early?"

Maya's eyes lit up. "Really? You have it here?"

Will nodded. "It's in there." He nodded toward the glove compartment. "It's not wrapped nicely or anything. But why don't you open it?"

He remembered watching her remove the small blue velvet box and opening it to find the delicate silver necklace with a little snowflake charm that had a diamond in the middle. Maya wore that thing for the rest of the year. Even after winter had long ended, that charm hung from her neck, even in the humid July weather as they lay out on beach towels under the sunshine.

"Are you really going to send that application to Chapman?" Maya had asked, her voice soft, scanning his face with a hint of hope in her eyes. "It's so far away."

"It's only for a few years," he replied, adjusting the charm on her necklace. "It'll fly by. You can visit, and I'll be home for the summers."

She was quiet, a distant look in her eyes. "You're going to meet so many interesting people. Do all these amazing things. And I'll be stuck here, commuting to Georgian College. Everything will be the same. Except you won't be here."

Will leaned forward, brushing a lock of hair from her face. "I might meet interesting people," he said, "but none of them will be you."

He kissed her. The storm's fury raged outside, but inside, everything felt suspended in time.

Twenty minutes later, a loud knock on the window broke the moment—thankfully, the snow had obscured the view—but Maya shrieked and scrambled to cover herself with her sweater while Will fumbled to pull on his jeans.

They'd stepped out of the truck to find that the sun had come out. They trudged through the fresh snowfall and picked out the perfect tree, leaving the farm feeling decidedly festive and full of hope for the future.

Now, he wanted to ask if she still had that necklace, but he knew in all likelihood it had ended up in the trash about twenty minutes after she'd received his text nine months later. He winced, thinking about how incredibly idiotic that move had been.

Why had he done it? What had allowed him to treat Maya, who'd been the center of his world for two of the most important years of his life, so callously?

The answer was simple. Because he'd known that if he called her and shared what was on his mind, the moment he heard her voice on the other end of the phone, there would be no way in the world he could go through with it. So instead of doing what he felt was the right thing—saving them both from a fruitless and impossible attempt at keeping their relationship going—he did what needed to be done.

He'd known in his heart that it would be a long time before he'd return to Sunset County. The weight of his father's disappointment and his anger toward the man—he couldn't picture going back.

He remembered pressing Send on his phone, then powering it down for the next twenty-hour hours. He couldn't bear to see her reaction when he felt just as torn up about it as he imagined she was. Everyone always felt badly for the dump-ee. But the dumper, he'd realized, with the added weight of guilt associated with the decision, was feeling equally, and maybe even more, crummy.

Now, they walked together down a grassy path with trees on each side, the sun beaming overhead. Today, Maya was wearing a gold necklace dotted with rubies. Her birthstone.

"What do you think?" Will asked.

"What do you mean?"

"I mean…what do you think?"

"What do I think about…climate change? The best variety of mango? Who should play the next Bond?"

Will laughed. "I'm interested in your thoughts about all of the above. But at this moment I'm interested in what you think about this as the setting."

Maya turned toward him and blinked. "I'm sorry. All this asking for my opinion all of a sudden… I'm feeling too important. Will I get a consultant credit on the film as well?"

"Don't joke," said Will. "I value your opinion."

For a second, Will thought Maya was going to frown and tell him all the reasons why she thought this was a substandard location. That it couldn't possibly live up to the image in her mind, even though he suspected that it was this very place she'd been thinking about when writing the scene.

But to his surprise, instead of hesitation, she parted her lips slightly and smiled. "I think… I think I really like it," she said, her eyes lighting up. "A lot."

Will nodded, a plan already forming. "We could get a shot of them cutting down the tree and hauling it to the truck."

"Show them starting to work together," Maya added, catching his rhythm.

"Exactly."

"Okay," she said with a thoughtful look. "Nice." Her eyes sparkled in the soft late afternoon light. "All this talk about Christmas trees has me craving peppermint hot chocolate."

He had been planning on taking her to see the building that was going to stand-in for the ski rental booth, but it would really only be a fifteen-second shot, and the idea of sitting together for a drink and talking held a lot of appeal.

"Think they have any at Rise and Grind?" asked Will. "We'd better get back there before they close."

Maya's smile widened. "Look at you. Getting into the Christmas spirit."

Will laughed. "I wouldn't go that far."

Chapter Fifteen

Maya carried the mugs over from the counter to the table Will was holding for them by the front window. The barista hadn't batted an eye when she'd made her order—apparently, they'd had a few over the past week, with all the Christmasy items on display in the town.

"Here you go," said Maya. "Hope you don't mind that I made the executive decision to add whipped cream."

Will accepted the mug that Maya slid across the table. "I'd be disappointed if you hadn't." He blew lightly on his drink. "So, one for two today, not bad." He took a sip of his hot chocolate, and Maya decided not to tell him he had an adorable micro dollop of whipped cream on his top lip. "I have to say, I kind of agree with you about the Greenwood estate."

"Really?" said Maya. "How so?"

"You're right. It's a little too…flashy."

Maya paused for a moment, letting the fact sink in that Will was actually taking her feedback. "I thought you dealt in flashy," she said.

"What do you mean?"

"I mean, that movie you made? About the art gallery heist?"

"Bonevo?" Will said.

"Yeah. That was like...conspicuous consumption on crack."

"Hold up," Will said. "What you're saying is you've watched my movies."

"One or two," Maya said. She sipped her hot chocolate, then wiped her own top lip, just in case.

"That movie demanded something flashy. It was about billionaires. I don't deal exclusively in flashy. I deal in authenticity. And I think you're right. The Greenwood estate is too swanky."

Maya nodded. "So what now?"

"Well, I'll call Shauna when I get back to the hotel and ask her to present me with some options tomorrow."

"Do I get to see them?" Maya asked.

Will paused, and he looked so deliciously handsome that it took everything in her not to lean across the table and kiss away that little bit of whipped cream. "I'd be happy to send them your way. But now I get to make a condition," he said.

Maya laughed. "Ohhh. Two can play at this game, I guess. Fine. What is it?"

"Do you have Thanksgiving plans?" Will asked.

Maya felt a tingle of pleasure at the impending invitation. "Normally I'd go to my parents' place, but they're getting ready to leave for Scotland with my aunt and uncle. So no. Bruce and I will probably watch *It's the Great Pumpkin, Charlie Brown* on my laptop and make ramen or something."

"That's...sad," Will said.

They both laughed.

"I can bake. But I'm a hopeless chef," Maya said.

"I don't get that," Will replied, leaning in slightly, his gaze locking with hers.

Maya felt a brief, almost magnetic pull to close the distance, but she held herself back, unwilling to let her desire show too obviously. "Baking is precise. Scientific. Follow the directions, and you're assured it'll turn out. Cooking is a little more...creative."

"What are you talking about? You're so creative," Will said. "You always have been."

Something twisted inside her stomach at his words. "That's you," she said. "I've just figured out how to follow a pattern. Writing romance is like baking, I guess." The second the words came out of her mouth, she regretted them. She didn't actually believe that. Of course romance was creative. She'd just listened to too many people denigrate the genre. And sitting across from Will, who was lauded as one of the most creative people in the world...no wonder the words had tumbled out.

"I don't believe that for one second," said Will. He put his mug down on the table and reached out, taking his hand in hers. "You're brilliantly creative. I admire the hell out of you."

Maya breathed in his words. "Thank you," she said. "Now what's the condition?"

"Come to my dad's for Thanksgiving dinner," he said. "I can't promise an amazing meal, but I can assure you that if you're looking for some conflict to sprinkle into whatever story you were working on when I picked you up this morning, you'll get some inspiration."

"I'd love to come to Thanksgiving dinner," Maya said. "Just tell me what to bring."

"I'll take care of dinner. And no, I won't be cooking.

But I'll order something in. Would you like to bring a dessert?"

Maya was already planning in her mind what would be the perfect thing to serve for Will and his father. Maybe a classic pumpkin or pecan pie. Nothing fancy, just tradition done right. Or something more elevated? Pumpkin cheesecake with gingersnap crust? Apple and pear galette? Chai-spiced pear cake with brown butter frosting?

When she looked up, Will had a funny expression on his face. "You've gone somewhere in your head," Will said, chuckling.

"Sorry," Maya said, smiling. "Just thinking about some options."

"Like I said." Will grinned. "You're the artistic type. Anyone who zones out of a conversation like that has more than one creative bone in their body."

"I'll bring something great," said Maya, a sudden warmth flushing her cheeks. "Just let me know when to show up."

"Happy hour snacks?" said Grace as Will entered the Briarwood. She was passing through the front foyer with a tray of pretzel bites and different kinds of nuts in small bowls.

He hesitated, then checked his watch. "Whatever those are smell amazing," he said.

Grace grinned. "Lily's been napping well these days, so I've been able to do some cooking, rather than offer drinks. What can I get you to drink?"

"I'll grab a beer if you've got any," said Will.

"Have a seat in the front room."

"No big rush," said Will.

Three minutes later, Grace placed a glass of pilsner in front of him along with an appetizer plate with a napkin. "Help yourself," she said. "Can I get you anything else?"

"This is great," said Will. "Actually, any chance you have a minute to chat?"

"Of course," said Grace. "Your crew's already been through, and the other two rooms have already checked in."

Will took a bite of the warm pretzel. "Mmm," he said. "Unreal." He shuffled through the pages on his clipboard. "I just came back from a location scout. My team's secured the locations for the key outdoor scenes, but something didn't sit well with one of them today. They've already arranged the permits and everything, but it never hurts to ask the locals to weigh in. Any chance I can pick your brain?"

"Ohhh, sounds intriguing," Grace said. "But aren't you a local?"

"I was, once upon a time," he said. "But as much as some things have stayed the same, a lot has changed."

Grace nodded. "Well, I've only been a local for three years now, but I'll do my best."

"Thank you," said Will. "Christmas tree farm?"

Grace considered. "There's the actual Christmas tree farm. Morton's?"

"Good. That's what we have in the books." He wasn't planning to move that location—Maya had been happy with it—but he wanted to make sure Grace could pass the good taste test. But the Greenwood estate was a no-go. He wanted to find something that would make Maya happy.

"How about a home that would look...really Christmasy all decorated?"

Grace's eyes brightened. "I mean, it's not a house, but the inn always looks pretty over the holidays."

The inn. Of course. Why hadn't he thought of that? "You'd be okay with that?" said Will. He thought about the large windows, cedar shingles, stone chimney and the heavy oak door. The inn was traditional. Classic.

"Most of our guests are associated with the film shoot. And the other couple of rooms would probably find it fun to see a movie shooting at the front of our hotel."

"I'll take it to my team," said Will.

Grace nodded toward his plate. "Can I get you anything more?"

"All set," said Will.

He spent Sunday morning reviewing the plans for the week with Shauna—who gave the Briarwood her enthusiastic seal of approval as a backup location. Afterward, he visited Pinecrest Haven to finalize Gene's move and settle the payment details. Once he returned to the inn, he snapped a photo of the front of the building and sent it to Maya.

How's this for Garrison Creek Lodge? he typed. Within moments, a string of heart-eyed emojis lit up his screen.

Will couldn't help but smile to himself. It was the right call for the film, but seeing Maya's reaction made him feel...well, really good.

Chapter Sixteen

The shoot at the Christmas tree farm was smooth and uneventful on Thanksgiving Monday, which gave Will more than a few occasions to linger in some flashback moments from all those years ago. Thoughts he shouldn't have been entertaining during a work day.

The fact that Maya was nowhere near set that day was the only thing allowing him to hold on for dear life to some degree of focus. He had to make sure Ben's sawing of the tree trunk was realistic and the placement of the tree in the back of the pickup underneath the rapidly falling "snow" was just so.

The day flew by, and they were able to wrap shortly after six o'clock. Will picked up dinner for three and drove out to Robin Point Road, where Gene was dozing in front of the television.

He put the take-out containers in the oven to stay warm, then fixed his hair in the bathroom mirror.

At seven o'clock on the dot, Will opened the door to find Maya, a white baker's box in each hand, sparkly pumpkin earrings dangling from her earlobes. They were so horribly unfashionable, like she was a grade school teacher dressing up for her students' sake, but somehow Maya made them look cool.

She noticed him checking them out. "I had to dress for the occasion," she said, handing him the bakers boxes.

"Now I feel underdressed," said Will, looking down at his jeans and crew neck sweatshirt. "I forgot to wear my pilgrim's hat."

"No," she said quietly, grinning, "you look really great."

The compliment danced across his skin, and suddenly he wished that instead of them about to sit down to dinner at his childhood home, across the table from his cranky father, he could take Maya to his favorite restaurant in New York, with the dim lights and candles and Motown playing over the sound system. They'd order a bottle of good red, a plate of oysters and linger over tapas.

Instead, it was a last-minute order from the BBQ joint on the highway leading to town: pulled pork, ribs and brisket with a side of coleslaw, baked beans and cornbread. Agatha had put out some cloth napkins and set a jug of homemade cider from one of the local farm stands on the stove to warm so that they'd have something festive to drink.

It wasn't Le Bernardin, by any measure, but it all smelled pretty darn good.

Will led Maya to the kitchen, where he deposited the boxes.

"I feel like I've walked out of a time machine," she said, eyes scanning the kitchen. He watched as her face lit up, and she clapped a hand across her mouth to stop the laugh from escaping. "Oh my goodness. The Elvis clock is still here."

It was probably the only item in the home that was uncharacteristically Gene: an Elvis Presley clock, with the singer in his iconic pompadour hairstyle, flashy seventies jumpsuit and rocking hips that replaced the standard pendulum.

"Think we should take that down before the viewings?" Will asked.

"Most definitely not," said Maya. "Talk about a unique selling feature."

"Want to come back and say hi to the old man?" Will asked.

But Maya was already through the door, and he stood listening, unable to keep the smile from spreading across his face as Maya greeted Gene.

"Hi, Mr. Hastings!" her voice rang out. "Look at you looking all fall chic in that houndstooth sweater! You definitely nailed the mood board. I haven't seen you in months!"

He couldn't make out what Gene was mumbling, but his tone had changed. It was soft, tender. Maya made his father melt into a gooey puddle the same way she did Will.

Will poured three mugs of cider and brought them to the living room to find Maya on the ottoman facing Gene, holding his hands in hers.

"I think you'll like the dessert I brought," she said. "Not the lemon Danish this time. But I tried something new, just for the occasion."

Will set two mugs down on the coffee table and one beside his father on a coaster. "Here you go, Dad," he said. "Hot apple cider. From Agatha."

Maya raised an eyebrow, teasing. "Is that your lady caller?" she asked with a mischievous grin. "Do tell!"

Gene rolled his eyes but couldn't hide the smile tugging at the corners of his mouth. "No, no lady caller. She has the much less glamorous job of helping me to the toilet," he said, chuckling.

"Come on, Dad," Will said. "You always said no crass talk over dinner."

"Or ever," said Gene.

Maya's easy laugh and presence filled the room, as if she had gently swept away the weight of the past few days. In that moment, it was like all the tension had dissolved, drifting away with the soft scent of her perfume and the warmth of her.

They chatted easily over dinner. Gene didn't eat much and seemed to move in and out of the conversation like a wave lapping at the shore, with the late evening sun spilling into the space. Maya regaled them with stories from culinary arts school. It was easily the best Thanksgiving that Will could ever remember.

"Happy Thanksgiving," he said, holding up his glass.

"And you get another one in what—six weeks?" Maya said, clinking her glass against his.

Six weeks. Where in the world would he be in six weeks? Far away from Sunset County, back at his place in Brooklyn. Or in Studio City, trying to find an investor for his new project.

He took a sharp breath in, trying to come to terms with the knowledge that wherever he was, Maya wouldn't be. And this moment, so steeped in nostalgia, would feel like a dream of the past, just like their time together in high school. The house would be in the hands of new owners, and Maya would be making her morning and evening walks to and from Flour Child, lighting up Sunset County in a way that he was certain no one fully appreciated.

"Okay," Maya said, after they cleared the plates and Will had gotten the correct answer for Final Jeopardy, "who's ready for dessert?"

"Let me help," said Will.

"You relax. That dinner must have taken ages to make!" she teased.

Will grinned. "I'm going to help."

In the kitchen, Maya used a knife to cut the tape securing the bakers boxes together. From the first, she slid a small tray of three crème brûlées, each with a mint leaf and a blackberry as garnish.

"Amazing," said Will. "You mean to say we're eating more than that?"

She pushed the second box toward him. "Just to be festive," she said.

Inside were three sugar cookies, iced in red, yellow and orange, all with sparkling colored sugar making the veins and grooves of the leaves.

"This is unbelievable," Will said. "We can't eat these. It's like…art."

"Edible art," Maya said. "And there's more where that came from. I made a big batch to sell this week. You can just be my taste tester."

Will looked up at Maya with amazement. "You're so crazy talented," he said. "Wow."

Maya rolled her eyes, a modest laugh escaping her. "Yeah, right," she said, her tone laced with self-deprecation. "Says the award-winning artist."

Will paused, taken aback by her words. "I don't know

what you're talking about," he said, his smile faltering for a second. "But everything I've seen—your bakery, your books—it's all so impressive."

Maya shrugged, a slight smirk tugging at the corner of her mouth. "Well, it's not like I'm a household name or anything," she said, her voice teasing but tinged with something else. "Mr. Bigtime."

There was an awkward shift in the air, and Will couldn't quite place it. He noticed the subtle bitterness in her words, something that seemed to linger beneath her playful tone. Something about his success, or perhaps the way he spoke about it, clearly didn't sit right with her.

He paused for a moment, considering whether to probe. But it had been a perfect evening up to this point, and he didn't want to ruin it. "You grab those plates," he said instead. "I'll bring the desserts in."

By the time they returned to the living room, Gene was sleeping in his chair. "I'll leave one out for him," whispered Will. "Agatha will be back soon to help him to bed. He might want it before he goes to sleep."

"Here," said Maya, tipping a crème brûlée onto his plate.

"You're not having one?" Will asked.

"Too much sugar for this close to my bedtime," Maya said. She glanced at her watch. "Speaking of which. I'd better go."

There was a subtle shift in the air between them since the moment in the kitchen, something unspoken that hung in the space. Will hesitated, torn between addressing it and letting it be.

He walked Maya to the front door and helped her on with her coat, then stepped outside with her into the cool evening. The smell of burning tamarack laced the air from a nearby bonfire.

"That was a lot of fun," he said. "And I've never once said that about a dinner with my dad."

"I'm glad I could come," said Maya. "And you do know your dad's a real softie at heart."

"Maybe to you," Will said. "He definitely has a soft spot for you."

Maya smiled. "Your dad loves you, too, you know. He's just not the best at showing it."

Will cleared his throat. "Anyway. We don't need to talk about that anymore. Are you sure you have to go already?" He was suddenly desperate for her to stay. Watch a movie on the couch and make popcorn. Sit outside by a bonfire of their own.

"I'd love that. But I need to let Bruce out. And those biscotti aren't going to make themselves tomorrow."

"All right," he said reluctantly. "Another week on Main Street. Glad you'll be around."

"Me, too," she said, and for a moment, the air between them felt thick with something unsaid. Will wanted to kiss her, more than anything in that moment.

Before he could gather his thoughts, Maya stepped closer, her face illuminated by the soft glow of the porch light. Without a word, she leaned in.

The feel of her lips against his took his breath away. Instinctively, he slipped his arm around her waist, drawing her closer as their lips met in a slow, lingering kiss.

He inhaled deeply, the sweet scent of strawberries in her hair mixing with the faint taste of icing still lingering on her lips, and for a moment, everything else faded.

Maya pulled back just enough to look at him, the air

between them still charged with the heat of their kiss. "Thank you," she murmured. "I had a great night."

Maybe he had read too much into her comments in the kitchen. Will gently held her hand, unwilling to let go just yet, wanting to savor every second of the moment. "Me, too," he said. "Get home safely, okay?"

Maya nodded, then paused as she turned to step down the porch stairs. She stopped halfway, a smile tugging at her lips as she looked back over her shoulder. "I'm having déjà vu," she said.

Will couldn't help but laugh. "Except tonight, you're the one setting your own curfew."

Her grin, the kind that made his heart skip a beat, widened. She pulled her keys from her pocket and slid into her car, tossing a final glance over her shoulder. "See you in the morning."

He stayed on the porch long after her car had disappeared, his eyes lingering on the spot where her taillights had faded, a quiet smile still playing on his lips.

Chapter Seventeen

Will rolled over at the sound of his alarm. It was the one thing that stayed consistent in every different bed he woke up in. Over the past two years, he'd only stayed at his Brooklyn condo two hundred and eighteen nights (he'd counted, in a moment of true boredom during a delayed layover at DCA, and when contemplating whether to sell the place and buy something smaller, given that he was never there). But no matter if he woke up in Jakarta or Queensland or North Dakota, always early, as his call sheet demanded, the light sound of jazz notes felt a little bit like home.

This morning, he was tempted to tap the snooze button on the screen and burrow deeper into the cloudlike duvet. But today was a big day.

He sat up. A big day indeed. Today was the day when he would direct his very first, and surely last, rein-dog parade. In order to muster up the energy required for the day ahead, he had to be optimistic. Embrace the lunacy of it.

Not lose his edge under Maya's prying eyes.

He groaned, thinking of the gorgeously mischievous look in her eyes when she'd handed him the signed copy of his book after the book club meeting. How she'd dropped to the edge of his mattress and how much he'd hoped she'd stay on that mattress, and that he wasn't in this empty bed thinking about his high school girlfriend and the many ways she was threatening to undo him, to throw him off his game in what really should be a blowout game but now felt like a real challenge.

Not only was Maya doing crazy things with his head, and to be very honest, much more than his head, but now he was staring down a full day of wrangling a whole new cast of furry characters and make some movie magic.

He gathered his things and exited the inn to where the production vehicle was idling. Usually, he was excited to jump into the car and be ushered to set, where a full day of creative problem-solving, high energy and flurry of activity awaited him. But for the first time since his early years, when he'd been determined to prove himself and be taken seriously, he felt a flicker of nerves at the pit of his stomach.

"Hey, Ivan," he said to the driver as he got in the back seat.

"All set?" Ivan said. "Quite the scene on set right now."

"I'll bet," said Will. Nerves were okay, right? A healthy amount of stress, to remind you that you cared?

He cared. He actually did care. This film was slowly becoming less of a joke, less of something to keep him busy while he tended to his father's business.

Now he found himself wanting to make it great. A holiday classic.

Not just for his résumé, but for Maya.

"Don't let any of those snobby professionally trained dogs make you feel any less than the superstar we both know you are," Maya cooed at Bruce. He was wriggling in her arms, dying to get down on the ground and sniff the other pups who were milling around in a fenced-off section on Main Street.

The four other dogs—a poodle, a chocolate Lab, a beagle, and a little Chihuahua in a red sweater named Worf were under the supervision of a handler named Susan. The middle-aged woman eyed Maya suspiciously, as though she and Bruce were new kids on the dog-for-hire block, intent on cornering her hard-won market with no training.

She would soon realize they had no business being anywhere near this film, especially when Maya considered Bruce's behavior over the last several days: chewing the strap of her brand-new purse, eating the rest of the burrito she'd been planning on saving for lunch the next day right off the coffee table when she left the room for two seconds to get her phone, and leaving her a yellow puddle of a gift right outside the bathroom door when she wouldn't allow him in while she was showering.

But what he lacked in professional training and acting experience, he more than made up for in cuteness. Maya placed Bruce on the ground and unhooked his leash, then watched in horror as he immediately approached the regal-looking shepherd and promptly began sniffing its backside.

"Bruce," she hissed. Why couldn't he play it even a little bit cool?

Just as she was about to call him over, the wardrobe supervisor and her assistant approached the pen. One of them held a small stack of headbands, each with a set of antlers attached. The other woman held a pile of folded leather leads with tiny silver bells attached that jingled as she separated them.

"Okay," said Kristina, the wardrobe supervisor. "Each of you cuties is about to transform into a majestic Christmas reindeer!"

"We're ready to film already?" said Maya. Poor Bruce probably needed just a minute to get accustomed to this new environment.

"We'll just check to see that these all fit okay," said Kristina. She craned her neck over to the set, where a couple of gaffers were fixing some lighting stands and the props department was fussing over Santa's sleigh. Santa sat under a tent a few feet away, his beard hanging under his chin from an elastic, his black boots up on a chair as he leafed through a magazine. Hopefully none of the local children would wander by and forever associate Santa with this decidedly unmagical moment.

Maya watched as one by one, the other dogs heeled obediently at their trainer's command and easily accepted the antlers placed on their heads. They continued sitting as Kristina made adjustments, then scratched them behind the ears for their good behavior.

"And last but not least, Bruce!" she exclaimed.

Bruce, embarrassingly, was now onto his third bottom—he was more than acquainted with the rest of his fleet now. When he noticed Kristina coming toward him with the antlers, he stopped for a moment, cocked his little furry head sideways, then darted to the other side of the pen.

"I'll grab him," said Maya. She moved to the other side of the pen. "Come here, baby," she said.

Bruce made a beeline to Maya and hopped into her

arms. She glanced up at Susan, hoping to catch a look of reluctant approval on her face at the sight of how Bruce took her command, but she was busy taking photos on her phone of the other dogs wearing their antlers.

Maya picked up Bruce and brought him to Kristina. Over her shoulder, she noticed Will watching from the monitor bay, a look of pure amusement in his eyes.

"Here we go," said Kristina, placing the headband on Bruce's head and fastening the little strap under his chin. He continued to wriggle, but Maya held him steady. "Let's see how this handsome man does with them while he's walking."

The moment Maya placed Bruce back on the ground, he darted to the closest fence and started rubbing his head on the fence posts in an attempt to knock the headband off.

"Bruce, honey, don't do that," Maya said, rushing over and picking him up again, then straightening the antlers. She grinned at Kristina, who now wore a dubious expression on her face. "He just needs to get used to them," she said.

Maya adjusted them a bit more, and when she looked up, Will was standing on the other side of the fence.

"How's our debut actor?" he said, his eyes still dancing with a kind of *I told you so* satisfaction. "Is he ready to learn the blocking?"

"I've already done a few walk-throughs with the others," Kristina piped up. "They're ready to hit their marks."

"Bruce here will just follow along," Maya said. And if he did, it would be a Christmas in October miracle.

"I just got the five-minute warning from Shauna," Will said. "You sure he's up for this?"

"Absolutely," said Maya, flashing her winningest and most confident grin.

"Let's get these cuties lined up," said Kristina.

By some miracle, Bruce allowed Kristina and her assistant to fit him in the leather harness. Once all the dogs were outfitted, Kristina connected them in a line with the other leather straps.

"Could this be any cuter?" said Maya, her heart brimming with pride at how well Bruce was doing, despite the rocky start. She slid her phone out of her pocket and took a few close-ups of Bruce, and then of the whole lineup. It went according to size, starting with the Chihuahua and ending with the Lab.

"Ready on set," a voice came through Kristina's mic.

"Rein-dogs traveling," responded Kristina. She placed the mic on her belt loop. "It's go time!"

Maya followed behind as Kristina and Susan led the group to the set, then positioned them in front of Santa's sled and clipped them in. Susan offered her four dogs treats for their good behavior. Why hadn't Maya thought of that?

Susan looked up from her dogs, which now appeared to be posing to be painted by an artist. Bruce was the only one not sitting. He was straining a little against his harness, but he wasn't barking or anything. So far so good.

"Okay if I stick close by?" said Maya.

Will nodded. "Please do."

He held her in a smoldering gaze, locking eyes a little longer than necessary, and Maya melted a little. Not only did she now have permission to be on set, but it seemed he wanted her there.

And as she watched him turn back to his crew and explain the shot composition and camera movement, Maya felt an overwhelming wave of attraction from seeing Will in action, not only because he was so assertive, confident and self-assured, but the seriousness in his voice and the detail with which he'd thought about this shot.

They were five cute puppies and a fairly lackluster Santa actor (luckily he didn't have any lines, so a good smile and wave would suffice), but in that moment, it was like Will was approaching the scene with the intensity of a director orchestrating a sweeping cinematic masterpiece. He might have been guiding the horses through the snow-dusted Russian countryside in *Doctor Zhivago*.

As soon as Susan gave a whistle (which, Maya knew now, would be removed in post), her dogs would begin walking. The dolly camera would follow them slowly at ground level, lingering for a moment on each one before panning up to Santa, who was waving at the parade goers.

Blake and Ginger were in the crowd. Later, when their close-ups were filmed, Blake would lean over to Ginger and ask her if she'd "brought her letter for Santa."

"All I want for Christmas is to pull off this wedding," Ginger would say in return. It was the line that would get Ben, who was now totally falling for Sarah, to resolve to do anything in his power to help make that happen.

As the lighting techs made final tweaks and Stu made a few adjustments to the placement of the extras lining the streets acting as parade goers, Maya experienced a rush of joyous positivity. This might just be the movie of her dreams.

And when Will called action, clear and steady through the cool October air, Maya clasped her hands in her chest. In clockwork perfection, the dogs started to move (as the third dog in the line, Bruce really had no choice but to comply), the camera operators had the dolly gliding down the tracks at perfect speed, Santa waved with all the equanimity that his role demanded, and Ginger and Blake glowed from the other side of the road.

"Cut!" Will called. Maya watched as he removed his baseball cap and ran his fingers through his hair. "Let's reset, but this time I want a tighter shot on the dogs and a slower pace on the movement. Let's keep it smooth."

The production crew slowly pulled the sled back into its original position, and with a series of snaps and kissing sounds, Susan directed the dogs to move as a group. Little Bruce was caught in the middle, once again with no option but falling in line. He let out a few cute little yelps, but overall, he'd done a great job on the first take.

"Nice work, baby!" Maya called, then looked over at Will, who was shaking his head lightly and smiling.

Minutes later, they were rolling again. The dolly started its movement, but Bruce was less willing to be in motion. He sat on the ground, and Worf and the beagle strained to pull him, while the larger dogs had to dodge him by going left and right.

"Cut," Will called, light resignation in his voice.

Dammit, thought Maya. It had all been going so well. They would try again, and Bruce would bounce back. She took a few steps toward the dogs but was too far away to prevent what happened next in seemingly a matter of seconds.

Bruce swiped his antlers against the retriever and somehow wriggled free from his harness. Before anyone could react, Bruce bolted down Main Street like he was running the Olympic hundred-meter dash.

"Bruce!" Maya yelled, her heels clicking against the pavement as she tried to chase him, but her shoes weren't exactly built for speed.

She heard a few other crew members call his name. As she continued to chase him down the fictional parade route toward the water, she watched as a few of the extras did their best to stop him, but Bruce was too nimble.

"I've got him," a voice called from behind her. Will was suddenly at her side, passing her quickly as he sprinted at top speed after Bruce.

Maya slowed her pace but kept going, following them down to the water.

Bruce had never been near the docks before. While Maya knew all dogs had a natural instinct for swimming, there were all kinds of boats and watercraft taking advantage of this glorious autumn day—who knew if they'd see Bruce or be able to avoid him if he leaped from the dock—which Maya could tell was his intention in the moment.

"Bruce, stop!" she shouted, but he was running so quickly she thought he might just start to fly.

What happened next was, well, a scene right out of a movie.

Bruce did indeed leap right from the dock into the frigid waters of Hollyberry Lake. He stayed at the surface, paddling, but the soft wind was blowing gentle waves away from the shore, and she could tell he wasn't yet strong enough to make his way back.

"Bruce!" she called again, her eyes filling with tears. She couldn't handle losing another dog in the space of a year. It would destroy her.

How had she ever decided to put him in this movie? Or course he wasn't ready. He barely knew how to heel. And it was her vanity and desire to have an upper hand that had caused this to happen.

She watched from fifty meters away as Will kicked off his shoes, shrugged off his jacket, then without hesitation, jumped into the water and did a head-up front crawl toward Bruce, padding his little paws in the water.

Maya ran out onto the dock and dropped to her knees, watching as Will grabbed hold of Bruce and held him at the surface while he kicked back to the dock. Maya waited until they approached and then reached down to grab Bruce, soaking wet with freezing cold water. He let her cradle him right against her chest. "You're okay," she gasped.

Will used the ladder affixed to the dock to hoist himself out of the water. His long sleeve shirt and jeans clung to his body as he brought himself to a sitting position on the dock's wooden planks.

Shauna wasn't far behind Maya, with Cam, a production assistant and Stu in tow.

"Are you okay, Will?" Shauna said. "Go get some towels," she said to the assistant. "The water's freezing."

"It's all right," said Will, but the assistant had already taken off up the street. "Just glad everyone's all right."

A small crowd had gathered at the shoreline, with

a few Sunset County residents aiming their cameras at them.

"Just smile," said Will through gritted teeth. "We don't want PETA knocking down our door with any suspicion of animal abuse on our set."

Maya grinned, and while part of it was forced—her heart was still pounding from exertion and the fear of losing Bruce—part of it was from elation that he was safe in her arms and that Will had saved him.

The assistant returned, out of breath and extending a pile of quilts. "These are—" he huffed "—for the fireplace scene. So we can't get rid of them."

"I'll make sure they get back to set," Will said, standing up and pulling the blanket around his shoulders. His lips were turning blue, but as always, he was as cool as a cucumber. Save for the fact that he was dripping a big puddle on the dock, no one would know that he'd just executed a heroic puppy rescue.

Shauna pulled her radio from her belt. "We're breaking for at least an hour," she said into the mic.

"No, I'm ready–"

"You need to get changed and warm up," Shauna said sternly. "You're no good to us if you've got pneumonia. Go back to the inn, take a hot shower, get changed, then we'll be back in business."

"All right," said Will. He looked at Maya. "Are you getting him home, too?"

Maya nodded. "Although—will you need him back on set?" she asked weakly. But she already knew the answer.

Will opened his mouth to respond, and then Shauna cut in. "Maya, you know I think Bruce is a darling, but it might be best…"

"If we do a little training before we sign on for our next role," Maya said. She sighed and looked down at Bruce, who was snuggled up in her jacket. He'd soaked her dress. The fact that she was starting to catch a chill meant Will must be absolutely freezing.

"I'll call the production van down here and get you both home," Shauna said. She moved away to continue talking on her mic.

"I'm sorry," Maya said to Will. "I should never have asked to include Bruce. That was really stupid of me."

"Don't sweat it," Will said. "I probably should have said no in the first place."

"But you didn't want me breathing down your neck."

Will paused. "Actually," he said, but before he could continue, the black production van was backing up toward them.

It came to a stop and the driver rolled the window down. "Where to first?"

"The Briarwood Inn," said Maya.

"No, we'll go to your place first," said Will.

"The inn," said Maya. "You need to get back on set. And Bruce is staying warm."

"All right," said Will.

A few minutes into the drive, Will's phone rang. "Sorry," he said. "I should get this. It's my agent."

"Of course," said Maya.

"Richard," said Will. "How's it going?"

Maya looked out the window as Will caught up with his agent, another person in his life who was obviously important but existed as a figment in her imagination.

She thought about Will's life at home. Who did he spend time with on weekends? Did he have people he met regularly for brunch? Who did he celebrate his birthday with? Call when he needed something? It occurred to her that as much as she felt like she knew Will—who he was at his core, his history—she knew little to nothing about this new Will. His world was a complete mystery to her.

"If he's willing to do that, I mean…" Will glanced at Maya, his expression one of dubious excitement. "We're wrapping after Friday for a couple of days. So the timing couldn't be more perfect." He paused, the nodded. "Yeah, a few minutes outside of town, I think. Let me just check on something and get back to you," he said, maintaining eye contact with Maya as they pulled into the Briarwood. "Any plans this weekend?" Will asked.

"Walk Bruce. Bake pastries. Sell pastries. Walk Bruce. Write the scene where Talia tells Garrison there's no hope for them. Walk Bruce. Go to bed?" Maya said. "Why?"

Will hesitated. "This is kind of crazy. But there's a big party out on Aspen Cove. A fiftieth birthday party for the guy who's financing a huge new franchise. He's asked me to come and meet with him about it. He's a bit of an eccentric and wants me out there to pitch him in person. He likes things to be…organic."

"Aspen Cove?" Maya said. "As in, the island off the coast of Newfoundland?"

"Apparently there's some kind of crazy hotel there. He's rented out the whole thing."

"Okay," said Maya, unsure where she came into the equation.

"Come with me," Will said. "It's just for the night."

Maya nearly recoiled at the thought. "Just for the night? That'll take forever to get there." She quickly calculated in her head: two hours to Toronto Pearson, another two hours waiting in the terminal, then a three-hour flight, followed by a ferry or another connecting flight to the island. It would be a full day of travel, just to turn around and come right back.

Will cleared his throat. "This financier? Jeff Lafontaine?" He paused and dipped his chin slightly. "He's a... man of means. He's sending a plane."

"Sending a plane?" Maya repeated, blinking. "I'm sorry, did you just say he's *sending a plane*?" She stared at him, half in disbelief. *Who sends a plane?* For a moment, she felt out of touch—like she didn't belong in this world where private jets and lavish trips were just... normal.

"He's sending a plane to that little airstrip outside of town."

Maya's mind reeled. She knew the airstrip—some of the wealthier cottage owners used it to skip the endless traffic on Fridays after work. But the idea of stepping onto a private plane felt completely outlandish.

"It's going to be a big industry party. Maybe you can meet some people who'd be interested in your other books." He looked at her, pleading. "It'll be fun."

Maya considered. Could she actually do it? Close the bakery for a day, find someone to take care of Bruce?

For one day, she could have a life larger than her quiet existence in Sunset County. She could hobnob with financiers. Be with Will and pretend that she belonged in this world. Be...big.

Before she knew it, the words slipped out. "Okay. I'll come." She let out a nervous laugh, shaking her head at the absurdity of it all. She noticed the pleased expression spreading across Will's face.

"I'll send you the details," he said, clearly relieved.

Maya shook her head as they pulled into the Briarwood's driveway. "All right," she said. "Good luck finishing up the shoot day."

"I'm sure I can work with the first take we got of Bruce, by the way," Will said.

"Thank you," she said. "Not just for that. But for saving him. I don't know what I would do if…"

"I'm glad he's okay," Will said. "Later, Maya."

She watched as Will strode up the path to the inn. Before entering, he turned and waved, that meltingly handsome smile on his face before he disappeared through the door.

"Where to next?" asked the driver.

"Fourteen Edith Street," Maya replied, her voice steady despite the swirl of questions in her mind. Was she really doing this? Heading to some exclusive Hollywood party, flying there by private jet, no less? She hadn't even asked about sleeping arrangements—what kind of amateur was she? Closing the bakery on Saturday meant a full day of lost income, but if Will could really introduce her to people who might be interested in optioning her stories… Would she be crazy not to take that chance?

"What do you think, sweetie?" she whispered to Bruce, who was still nestled in her coat against her chest. "Has Mommy gone mad?"

Bruce licked her cheek, and she kissed him on the head.

"I'll just take that as a yes," she murmured.

Chapter Eighteen

"And that's a wrap," Will called late Friday afternoon. He was exhausted from the long shoot week, and they'd only gotten two of the three scenes they were meant to shoot that day. Paying overtime wasn't in the budget, so they'd be moving scene three to another day.

"What do you think?" Shauna said. "Can we cheat the fireplace scene? Shoot it up against the wedding dress pickup?"

Will considered. "I don't think so," he said. "We'll have already used those extras in a few scenes. It's going to be too obvious."

"I'm a bit concerned about the next block," said Shauna. "We're much too far behind where I'd like us to be."

Will nodded. "I agree. Any chance we can hit the tree farm and the hotel exterior on the same day?"

Shauna considered. "Might be a bit hectic. But I'll see if I can make it work."

"We just need to make sure we leave enough time for the ending," Will said. Which, he had to admit, was going to be a fun few shoot days.

The final scene of *Love on the Slopes* would be nothing short of legendary, as far as holiday romance movies went. With the wedding guests assembled at the bottom of the ski hill, one by one, the groomsmen would descend from the top of the ski hill, skiing gracefully down the snowy aisle, with the groom following closely behind in a flawless procession.

But just as all the guests craned their necks to see if the bride would follow suit or follow her six bridesmaids down the pink carpet runway rolled out from the lodge, there would be a twist in the plans. Once the bridal party was in place, the bride would make her entrance, not from the lodge, but from behind it, in a vintage horse-drawn sleigh. Her father would meet her and help her out and then walk her down the aisle.

However, a wrench gets thrown into the plans when the ski lift breaks down with Sarah on her way up to check on the groomsmen.

While she's suspended in the air, she and Ben have the fight that's been simmering the whole time she's been planning the wedding. He diminished her work. He's too cynical to even entertain the idea that a marriage could work out. And while he's built a successful business, he hasn't for a moment recognized that she's done something with her life, too.

Ben recognizes the error in his ways and confesses his love from below. The ski lift starts working again, he scales the "mountain" to be by her side, then helps her pull off the wedding.

Will was determined to make it a flawless cinematic moment, despite the heavy-on-the-cheese factor, but the two-day shoot at the ski hill needed to be tight. There was no room for error. The cost of operating the lift off-season, the snowmaking equipment required to transform the hill into a winter wonderland, the numerous extras and extensive wardrobe involved, and the horse-drawn sleigh brought in from Blue Mountain at an eye-popping cost—meant that there was no leeway for a third day. Every second was going to count.

"Thanks for everything, Shauna," Will said. "Make sure you take a break over the next couple of days. You deserve it."

Shauna raised an eyebrow. "I've got a spa day planned after we wrap. Until then, these logistics aren't going to sort themselves out. But in the meantime, there's that dark roast that's keeping me going," she said, nodding toward Rise and Grind. "I'll be hanging out there tomorrow."

"All right, I'm heading back to the inn. Call me if you need me," he said.

For a moment he wondered if he should be sharing his plans for the next couple of days, but he reconsidered. He'd text Shauna later and say he was leaving town for the days off, which was well within his right, but the idea of telling her where he was going felt off. He'd done a good job at this point downplaying the fact that the productions he usually worked on were tenfold the scale of this one. He feared that any talk of industry parties or private jets would only serve to disrupt the nice rapport he'd build with his crew, whom he'd grown to really like.

In fact, Will had to admit that the smaller scale of the set, the more pared-down crew, the absence of the weight of the massive studio expectations... He'd missed this.

And now he was on the way to convince Jeff Lafontaine to select him to direct what would be his biggest project yet. The prospect was equal parts thrilling and, if he had to be honest, maybe a bit exhausting.

After a quick shower, he sat at the table in his room, looking over his notes for his conversation with Jeff. Of course, they'd talk about *Infinite Realm*. But if Will saw any small opportunity, he wanted to float the idea of his Herman Melville biopic as well.

The shift in focus was jarring. One moment he was knee-deep in garland and tinsel, trying to decide how low a mistletoe should hang into the frame of a shot, and the next here he was, back in the world of massive soundstages and epic stunts, harpoons and raging seas and gritty tales of alcoholism and death. It felt strange, like parachuting between worlds.

Pitching another project when he was being brought out to talk about what was going to be a home-run box office smash was also risky. He had to be careful. He knew Jeff was a fan of his work, but the biopic would be a gamble. Still, something about being on this set over the past week, working with a smaller team and executing the vision of someone he cared about was giving him an itch to return to his roots.

When Richard had called in the production van the other day, Will hadn't even thought twice before inviting Maya to join him. A vision in his mind of the party, under dim lights, Maya wearing a dress, a luxury hotel on an otherworldly island... It was too inviting.

Framing the invitation as a networking opportunity hadn't been completely untrue—he'd introduce Maya to a few people, sure. But at its heart, he wanted her there with him because, more than he wanted to admit, any distance between them was starting to feel like a challenge.

So when his phone buzzed again, and he picked it up to find a message from Maya, his heart soared.

What time are you picking me up?

In the stillness of the morning, Maya searched around for her iPad charger. "Dammit," she exclaimed. She'd left it at the bakery, where she'd stayed late the night before to make sure the cases were full for Lucas that morning.

Will would probably have one, but she didn't want to take a chance.

"You wait here, baby," she said to Bruce and hopped in her car.

She pulled up quiet Main Street and was surprised to see the lights on already in the bakery. Had she forgotten to turn them off before locking up?

She entered what sounded like a nightclub, hip-hop music laced with expletives blaring through the speakers.

When she passed through the counter, she found Lucas, apron on, flour up to his elbows, kneading dough like he was punishing it.

"No need to press it right through the counter," she called over the music, and Lucas looked up, startled.

"I didn't think you were coming in today," Lucas said. He looked like he'd just been caught red-handed committing a felony instead of working out some bread dough. "I just—I wanted to practice what you showed me. Don't worry, I wasn't going to try to sell it or anything. I'll pay for the materials."

Maya turned down the music on the speaker, then approached Lucas's workstation and inspected the dough. "Looks pretty good, actually," she said. "You're up early today."

Lucas shrugged. "It's easier when I do it every day, rather than ruin my routine by sleeping in on the weekends."

Cassie would fall off her chair if she heard her son make such a mature observation, Maya thought. "Why don't you see how it comes out? If they look good, you can sell them for half price and keep whatever profits you make. You washed your hands like I showed you, right?"

"I did. And really?" said Lucas. "Okay. Wow, cool. Thank you." He dusted his hands off on a clean tea towel. "And I should have asked you before coming in early. I'm sorry."

Maya shook her head. "No apology needed. I gave you the keys, right? I trust you. As long as this party you're throwing in here remains a party for one, and if you clean up after yourself, I'm okay with you being in the space."

Lucas relaxed visibly. "Thank you."

"Thank you," Maya said. "If it weren't for you, I'd be stuck here all day instead of going to a fancy party tonight."

"Fancy party, eh," said Lucas, grinning. "You getting lit tonight?"

Maya laughed. "I don't even know what 'lit' is, so I'm going to say probably not." She looked back at the pile of dough on the counter. "Let that rest a little. And then you're ready to braid." She winked at him, grabbed her charger from under the counter and left Lucas, her little bakery miracle, alone with his dough.

Maybe her optimism was unchecked or maybe she was just caught in a cloud of excitement and nerves for the night ahead, but the funny thing was, she actually did trust him.

* * *

An hour later, Maya paced the hallway between her kitchen and bedroom, trying to work off some nervous energy. Will was due to arrive any minute, and she didn't want to appear overeager by hovering at the door. She double-checked her purse to make sure she had everything, then assessed her appearance again in the hallway mirror.

When the doorbell rang, her heart started to pound. Was she actually doing this?

She opened the door to find Will standing on the front porch, the production van idling in the driveway with Ivan in the driver seat.

Will eyed her suitcase in the corner. "Can I grab that for you?"

Maya nodded, then followed him out to the van. Even though she had spent the last few years just fine on her own, she had to admit that she was craving this type of attentiveness. He opened the front door for her, where she slid in and wished Ivan a good morning.

The drive to the small airport just outside of Sunset County was brief. Maya knew the airport existed but had never had a reason to visit. Now, as Ivan navigated the SUV onto the runway, where a gleaming plane with just six windows along the side sat waiting for them, she was starting to see the appeal to the way the other half lived. Being *sent a plane* was pretty darn fabulous.

A woman in a gray wool coat and high-heeled boots approached the van with a clipboard and greeted them warmly. "Mr. Hastings, Ms. Monroe," she said. "I'm Kari, and I'll be your flight manager today."

They shook hands with Kari, and she signaled to a

young man standing behind her to grab their luggage. "Eric will take your luggage. If you follow me, we'll check in over there in the building, then we'll be ready to take off in about twenty minutes."

Will motioned for Maya to go first, so she followed Kari toward the building and stole another glance at the jet. The *private* jet. The private jet that belonged to a bigwig in the entertainment industry and that she was about to hop on so casually while someone else handled her luggage. Was this really happening?

An image of the crowded airport she'd endured when traveling to Montreal for a friend's wedding several years ago flashed through Maya's mind. The lines, the screaming children, the disgruntled airline agents. Maya marveled at how civilized this process was.

Enjoy this, she reminded herself as they showed their identification and went through a basic security check.

Together, she and Will walked out toward the plane, where a set of stairs had been wheeled out to connect to the cabin.

They ascended the stairs, Maya first, then entered through the jet's narrow doorway.

Maya clapped her hand over her mouth to try to stifle the gasp that sounded as she stepped into the cabin. It was unbelievable that someone would have this at their disposal at any time. The inside of the aircraft matched the immaculate gleam of the exterior, with plush white leather seating, polished cherry tables with gold trim, dim lighting and soft classical music setting a calm ambience.

"Not too shabby," said Will from behind her.

"I'm afraid to touch anything," Maya whispered, taking in every detail of the plane. She couldn't help the laugh that escaped. She was no longer Maya Monroe. She was Marilyn, and Will was her John Huston.

"Well, don't worry about a thing. Put your feet up. Relax a little."

Maya sank into the buttery soft chair just as Kari entered the jet. Outside, the crew locked the door and began takeoff procedures. "May I get you some champagne?" Kari said, gesturing toward an ice bucket holding a bottle of Bollinger beside two thin crystal flutes.

It was only shortly after noon, but this was her first and likely last opportunity to drink bubbly on a private luxury jet. Maya sat back in the leather chair as Will accepted the flutes from Kari.

From a compartment underneath the ice bucket, Kari extracted a small tray piled with a selection of cheeses, fresh figs, paper-thin slices of prosciutto, bread and crackers. She placed it on one of the tables with some cloth napkins. "Lavatory is at the rear. Just push this button if you need me," she said, pointing to a call button on the wall near the table. Then she promptly disappeared behind a curtain toward the front of the plane, leaving them alone in the cabin.

Maya plucked a plump red grape from the plate and popped it in her mouth. "I can see the appeal to your lifestyle," she said.

"This isn't my lifestyle," he said. "I spend most of my time on set. And when I'm not on set, I'm in a dark editing suite, agonizing over color correction."

"Okay, Mr. Modest," Maya said. "I think you know just as well as I do that you run in glamorous circles. I've seen the tabloids."

"Don't believe everything you see online," Will said. "And you've always been the glamorous one." His gaze flickered over her. "She wore diamonds on the soles of her shoes," he sang softly.

A wash of pleasure ran through Maya's veins at the sound of the song Will used to sing to her any time he picked her up for a date and he could tell she'd taken time to get dressed to impress. How many times had she heard that familiar refrain? *Ta na na na*, she heard his voice in her head. *She wore diamonds on the soles of her shoes.*

They might have been young. But Will had been a natural romantic, and now as he picked up the flutes from the table so easily, his eyes sparkling with amusement, she could tell he still was.

He poured from the bottle and passed one to Maya. Their fingers brushed as she accepted it, and he seemed in no hurry to let go of his hold on the stem. Seconds ticked past, and Maya's pulse sped up.

"So," Will said, stretching out his legs in front of him, into the endless legroom that the layout of the cabin afforded them, "what made you decide to come? You seemed unsure."

He had shed his jacket and was sitting close enough that Maya could almost feel the warmth radiating from his body, from the dipping neckline of his button-down, sleeves rolled up to reveal his strong forearms and those hands, those hands that she longed to hold with hers. His deep brown eyes studied her intently as he awaited her response, the furrow of his brow leaving no doubt that what she said mattered to him.

You, she kept herself from saying. *You made me decide.* "I'm just glad to be here." She raised her glass to toast him. "And I appreciate you making some introductions. Who knows where this could lead."

He nodded. "Good."

The moment was interrupted when the engines began rumbling beneath them. Slowly, the jet started to taxi to the runway. Maya watched out of the small window as they slowed to a stop at the takeoff line. She felt Will come closer to her on the couch as he shifted to look out the window, and she shivered as she felt the warmth of his frame behind her. Their hands were touching on the couch as the jet picked up speed, the tree line out the window disappearing the farther they climbed. Neither moved.

"I meant what I said the other night, at my dad's," Will said. "You're really impressive."

She could feel his voice washing away some of her feelings of inadequacy, polishing up her confidence, lighting up her spirit. Closing her eyes, she let Will's words wrap around her like a blanket. She breathed deeply, willing him to continue, then looked up to face him.

His eyes locked on hers intently, full of desire.

"Thank you," she whispered. "That means a lot."

The higher they climbed in the sky, and the farther the distance became between Maya and her life in Sunset County, the more daring she felt, more free and more alive.

They sat together quietly, gazing out the window at the pillowy clouds drifting by. Maya breathed in the feeling, electricity coursing through every part in her body. If she could bottle up this feeling, she would, but for the moment, she was going to soak up every second of this fairy-tale day and do her best to keep a lid on the small but nagging feeling that whatever this was had a greater meaning for her than for Will.

In a week's time, the shoot would be over, and he'd be taking off on another plane, back to his big life outside of her small town. What would she be to him then?

When the jet descended through a clear, sunny sky and touched down at the Aspen Cove Aerodrome Airport, a small grounds crew was waiting to greet them. Maya spotted another black SUV. This type of production was so foreign to her, all the people waiting on them and ferrying them around.

Maya looked sideways at Will as he searched through his bag, trying to gauge if he felt the same way or if he had become desensitized to moments like this.

"Come here," he said, typing the passcode on his phone and putting his arm around her shoulders, pulling her in. "This deserves a selfie."

She was glad that there was still some novelty to the experience for him. She grinned as Will snapped a few pictures.

"Don't forget to send those to me," she said. "You know how to work angles."

He motioned for her to stand near the exit to the jet, where the stairs had been wheeled up and the door opened. "No," he said. "I just have the perfect subject."

She had no problem flashing a huge smile as he took her photo.

The ride to the Aspen Cove Inn was only fifteen minutes, barely enough time for Maya to take in the impressive landscape that surrounded them as they sped down the main highway of the island. Rocky plains spilled into the sparkling Atlantic Ocean, and quaint, brightly colored houses dotted the shoreline, overlooking a glittering iceberg in the distance.

Their driver pointed out local landmarks and shared some history about the area. The island was equal parts otherworldly and homey. If they'd been staying more than twelve hours, it would be an amazing place to explore.

The inn was an elegant but striking modern structure sitting atop craggy rocks on stilts that seemed to be offering it up to the deep blue sky. She had seen it in pictures, but in person, it was breathtaking.

"Think this'll do?" Will asked, his gaze locking onto hers with those deep brown eyes that seemed to see straight into her. In that moment, something inside her shifted. Maybe, just maybe, she wasn't as ordinary as she thought. Because right now, she felt larger than life.

"I think we'll manage," she said, sighing gratefully.

The lobby of the hotel was warm and inviting and bathed in natural light. Maya gazed out at the ocean view as they approached the front desk, wondering if anyone could ever get tired of such an amazing vista.

The front desk representative looked up from her computer and smiled. "Welcome to the Aspen Cove Inn. I hope your trip here was comfortable," the woman said. "Names, please?"

"Maya Monroe. I'm here with Will—"

"Ah, Mr. Hastings," the woman said. "I'm Erin. Mr. Lafontaine is pleased that you could both join us."

"We're thrilled to be here," Maya said. She noticed

a photo of two small girls on the background of Erin's computer and paused before picking up her bags. "Are those your children?" she asked.

Erin beamed. "Yes. Maisie and Nora," she said.

"They're beautiful," said Maya. "They look just like you."

"Thanks," said Erin, blushing. "I appreciate that. A handful but sweeter than pie." Her formality had decreased slightly. "Thanks for asking. Listen, you just see me personally if you need anything. I'll show you to your room."

Maya and Will followed her down the solid oak hallway, turning left and then left again until they reached the elevators. They stopped briefly around every corner to gaze at a new panorama of the ocean that seemed to greet them at every angle.

"Mr. Lafontaine has requested that his guests assemble in the restaurant at five thirty for cocktails," Erin said, while the elevator ascended to the third floor, which was the top level, "in time to watch the sunset. In the meantime, please feel free to relax and make use of the facilities. There's a rooftop Jacuzzi with a very special view of the ocean. Our concierge can arrange for a walking tour of the inn's grounds, highlighting our sustainability practices and local sourcing of our restaurant's cuisine."

The elevator doors opened, and at the end of the hall, Erin used a key card to unlock the door to the room, then slid it into a small paper envelope and passed it to Maya. "Or," she said, opening the door to their suite and revealing a picture-perfect floor-to-ceiling window view of the ocean, "you may just want to spend some time here. Welcome to the Cabot Suite, our finest room."

"What a dump," Maya joked as they entered the two-story, two-bedroom space. Views from all sides gave the illusion that they were standing outside while surrounded by gorgeous Scandinavian-style furniture. She tore her eyes away from the vista to see Erin crouched over, lighting a fire in the wood-burning stove. "Wouldn't Jeff—Mr. Lafontaine—want this suite?" she asked.

Erin stood up and smiled politely. "Mr. Lafontaine has rented out the full inn, but it's likely he and some of his friends will be departing at the conclusion of the celebration," she said. "He's also arranged to have the airport open overnight, for the convenience of his guests."

Of course, Maya thought. "Mr. Lafontaine" and his crowd would be hopping in their jets to return to their mansions or maybe to hit the next party in Miami or New York. Luckily for her. This room was a dream come true.

"Do you have everything you need?" Erin asked.

"And then some," Maya said, grinning at Will. Erin bid them farewell, then left them standing in the most beautiful space Maya had ever seen.

"This is so incredibly gorgeous," said Maya. She approached the floor-to-ceiling windows to gaze out at the ethereal landscape, the black jagged rocks of the shore kissed by sparkling, deep blue ocean. "Come see," she said.

She felt Will behind her. They stood looking out at the water for a moment before she turned to face him, taking in how the late afternoon sun reflected in his warm chestnut eyes.

The fire Erin had just lit was flickering, adding to

the honey light filling the suite with warmth. Maya felt drunk with the perfection of the moment and sank into the soft couch facing the windows.

"Why don't you relax for a bit?" Will said. "I'm going to go downstairs to the lounge and make a few phone calls. Shauna has some questions about Monday. You'll be here when I get back?"

Maya laughed. "They might have to haul me out of here kicking and screaming." She gazed up at Will, grateful and electrified and incredibly magnetized to him.

Will left, and Maya decided to have a bath while she waited for his return. Undressing on the second level in front of the expansive windows was a strange sensation, but unless a fishing boat happened to navigate by, only the birds would catch a glimpse of her naked body.

Easing into the hot water, Maya exhaled with pleasure, marveling at how only hours earlier, she was scrubbing the toilet of the bakery's bathroom. Now, gazing out at the vastness of the Atlantic Ocean, the stress and exhaustion of the last few weeks melted away into the warm bath, replaced with the anticipation of Will coming back to the room. She lay in a dreamlike state for twenty minutes, then decided to get out before Will returned.

She heard a gentle knock at the door and pulled her robe tight against her chest.

"Room service," a female voice called from the other side of the door downstairs.

Maya descended to the main floor and opened the door to find a young woman with a cart on wheels. Maya stepped aside to let her in.

"Good evening. I'm Ginny. I'll be serving your suite during your stay. Mr. Hastings asked me to send this up,"

Ginny said. "He told me to let you know he'll be back in ten minutes."

"Thank you," Maya said.

Ginny proceeded to lay out a selection of snacks on the living room table, then took out an ice bucket and two wineglasses. "Would you like me to uncork this for you?" she asked, holding up a bottle of what looked to be a very fine wine.

"Sure," Maya said, reveling in yet another thoughtful gesture from Will.

Ginny popped the cork, nodded politely at Maya, then left promptly.

In the space of four hours, the same elegant and indulgent action had happened twice in front of her eyes. It was all too much.

Maya plucked a chocolate-covered strawberry from the tray and flopped back onto the couch again. She loved the dress she'd brought for the party, but she could totally live in this robe.

The first bite of the strawberry was perfectly sweet. "Mmm," she sighed. She could *totally* get used to this.

Chapter Nineteen

Will made a few notes on Monday's call sheet, then glanced up through the entrance to the sweeping windows of the hotel's restaurant, where the guests would soon assemble for an elegant cocktail party. He watched the efficiency with which the hotel staff set up buffet stations and polished glassware at the bar.

He was ready to go back to the room and spend time with Maya before the party.

It was foreign but comforting to know that when he got back there, he wouldn't be all alone. Every now and then, he would spend some time with his crew members after a shoot day, but generally, he would be by himself in his room.

Now, he'd be returning to a gorgeous woman with a special gift for making people feel important. Will thought about how the eyes of the woman at the hotel's front desk had lit up when Maya expressed genuine interest in her children. How Erin had quickly shifted from pleasant and perfunctory to warm and open. Will took in a sharp breath as he imagined himself wrapped up in that care and attention.

He whistled as he got off the elevator, then knocked on the door and waited a moment before entering. Through the windows, he could see the sun beginning its dip toward the water. The light of the sun cast an amber glow throughout the room, and when he found Maya sitting on the couch, his heart skipped a beat. For a moment, he allowed himself to imagine this very image as a regular occurrence in his life.

"Hey," he said, joining Maya on the sofa, drawn to her magnetically. She was still wearing her robe, and he did his best not to concentrate on what was underneath it.

"How is everything looking downstairs?" she said.

"It's pretty unbelievable," he said. "I think it'll be a good party." But for now, they had precious alone time together, which he intended to savor. "We've got a few minutes before we're due downstairs. I'm going to grab a quick shower and change. Can I pour you a glass of wine?"

"Sure," Maya said, gazing out the window. Her soft red waves caught the sun, the strands practically glowing in the late afternoon light. "Just look at this. I could never get tired of this view."

He went to the table where the catering order had been delivered, poured her a glass of wine and brought it to her. He leaned over to kiss her softly on her cheek and felt her breathe in deeply at his touch. It was agonizing to tear himself away, but he was happy to know he'd be returning to this very spot with Maya later this evening. It couldn't come soon enough.

He smiled to himself as he scaled the stairs to the second floor, embracing the warmth that came with having someone here by his side.

While Will showered, Maya changed into the dress she'd brought for the party, a sleeveless navy-blue silk

A-line with gold sequined stars sewn all over it. She'd bought it for her cousin's wedding at a vineyard in Prince Edward County last spring. She stared out at the picture-perfect vista, listening to the sounds of Will getting ready upstairs. When she heard him descending the stairs, she straightened up.

"Everything okay?" he said, fastening his watch on his wrist. He stopped on the stairs when he saw her on the couch, his expression shifting. "Wow," he said. "You look…stunning."

"Thank you," Maya said, drinking in the compliment. "You've cleaned up well yourself."

His hair was tousled and damp, and the alluring scent of his bergamot cologne filled the space, at once calming and electrifying her as he took the spot next to her on the couch. Without a word, he leaned over and tucked a strand of hair behind her ear.

She closed her eyes as he closed the distance between them and kissed her gently.

Thoughts of her life in Sunset County disappeared, and all of a sudden Maya felt important, attractive, glamorous—she felt completely alive. Desperate for more, she leaned into the kiss, Will's soft groan fanning the flames of her desperate need.

He pulled back, breathing deeply, and fixing her in his gaze. "We should probably head downstairs soon," he whispered, smoothing a strand of hair back from her cheek. He kissed her again, softly, his lips lingering for a moment, telling her without words that he'd rather do anything but leave. She could have stayed for the rest of the night here with him, but he had a job to do. They'd be back in their suite soon enough.

"I'm ready," Maya said, her lips still humming with the sensation of his kiss.

Will stood up and offered his hand, and she allowed him to pull her up to her feet. "Stunning," he said again, his voice warm and admiring, a light smile tugging at the corners of his eyes.

Maya turned to grab the key card from the desk, Will took hold of her hand, and she turned back to face him.

"It really means a lot to me, having you here," he said quietly. "I hope that doesn't sound weird. Just usually…" He paused. "I love my work, but it's usually kind of lonely." He looked at her, attraction and intensity in his eyes.

"I'm glad," said Maya, her entire body pulsing with desire. This feeling between them—it was more than just physical. It was deep, tender and real.

Will leaned over and kissed her on the lips again, holding her waist and pulling her close.

Their lips moved together, slowly at first, then with a building urgency that made Maya tremble. She breathed in the intoxicating scent of his cologne, savoring the firmness of his chest as she trailed a hand from his shoulder down toward this abdomen, where she broke her touch and took his hand again. Tugging on it lightly, she pulled him back down to the couch without breaking the kiss.

Without a word, Maya lay back on the pillow and watched as Will shifted in his seat, then positioned himself over her. He held her in his gaze while slowly, he slid his hand along her thigh to where her bare skin met the hem of her dress.

His touch was electric, stoking the flame of her need

even brighter. Her breathing became more shallow as she drank in the focused desire in his eyes.

"I think we can be fashionably late," she breathed, placing her hand over his and encouraging him to travel farther up her thigh.

Will said nothing, but his touch felt like a conversation, a declaration of everything he hadn't said but that he wanted. It told her in no uncertain terms that he'd forgotten all about the pitch, and the only thing in the world that mattered was making love to her.

"You think so?" he finally said in her ear, the warmth of his breath and depth of his voice eliciting a sigh of pleasure from her. He trailed light kisses on the soft skin of her neck, sending sparks traveling across her skin to where she ached for his touch.

"Mmm-hmm," Maya breathed as Will gently tugged her dress. She arched her back to indicate she wanted it off.

The silk slid easily over her head as she helped Will pull it off, then her bra, and in a moment, she was lying back as he scanned her naked torso, luxuriating in the feeling of being appreciated by a man who was an expert in aesthetics. The dreamy gaze of desire in his eyes was unmistakable. He was pleased with the scene in front of him.

"I want you," Maya murmured, her voice thick with need.

Will shed his shirt, the fading sunlight casting a warm glow over his toned frame. He smiled, his eyes softening. "Maya, you have no idea."

Chapter Twenty

By the time they descended to the party, a crowd had assembled in the dining room, which was filled with the rich rose-gold light of the sunset's finale.

Maya's entire body was buzzing with satisfaction. She was almost lightheaded, as though she was walking through a dream. Making love to Will bore no resemblance to the inexperienced, hurried and stolen moments of their youth. Will was skilled, attentive and patient to have his own needs met.

Now, Will's hand remained at the small of her back as they entered, a quiet gesture that still sent a spark through her, even through the fabric of her dress. She couldn't help but shiver, recalling the way his touch had felt—purposeful, tender and leaving her with a sense of being cherished, seen and utterly alive. It was as though she were floating on a wave of something she couldn't quite define but which made everything feel possible.

Waiters passed through the room with trays of champagne and cocktails, offering an extravagant array of hors d'oeuvres: caviar and crème fraîche tartlets, shrimp toasts with sesame seeds and scallions, and feta, beet and persimmon in delicate endive cups. There was an entire table with multiple levels of freshly shucked oysters on beds of glistening shaved ice. A line had formed next to the carving station, where a member of the restaurant staff shaved pieces of roast beef onto small plates, with fresh horseradish and grainy mustard as toppings.

Scanning the crowd, Maya noticed that there was a sheen to everyone in attendance. Beautifully tailored outfits with demure but expensive-looking fabrics, glittering jewelry and perfectly styled hair and makeup—young and old, everyone looked as though they had walked right off a runway into the party.

She looked down at her outfit. It was nice enough, but suddenly she felt underdressed compared to everyone else in the room. She tugged at the hem of her dress, then straightened her shoulders, trying to project as much confidence as she could.

A statuesque woman breezed by carrying a handbag Maya knew cost over five thousand dollars. *You've got diamonds on the soles of your cute Mary Jane flats*, she reminded herself. More like cubic zirconias.

"There's Jeff," Will said under his breath. She traced his line of sight across the room to the man she guessed was Jeff Lafontaine, flanked by two women. One of them was a statuesque model that Maya recognized from the society pages of the newspaper.

"Don't leave me alone, all right?" Maya said. "I feel out of place. Underdressed."

Will gave her hand a reassuring squeeze and turned his gaze on her, his expression full of warmth. "You look unbelievable," he said, his voice low and sincere.

"Easy for you to say," Maya whispered. "People expect you to show up anywhere in jeans and an ironic T-shirt. You're famous enough to get away with it."

"Just stick with me, and no one will even bat an eye," Will said.

Maya bristled. Of course, she liked that he was trying to make her feel better, but was he insinuating that without him, she'd stick out at the event? She did her best to push the feeling aside. The evening had been perfect so far, and Will was going to introduce her to some contacts in the industry. She had to be on her A game. She could be irritated with him later.

"Shall we get a drink?" Will said.

A drink. Yes. A drink was a good start.

She followed Will to the bar, where a bartender was straining something from a cocktail shaker.

She accepted a ruby red cocktail from a waiter and took a long sip. The sweet berry flavor calmed the anxiety that was suddenly washing over her.

"I know I said stick with me," Will said, his attention back on the other side of the room. "But I just need a sec to say hi to Jeff. You okay?"

Maya held up her glass. "Go get 'em," she said, then melted a little as Will flashed her the most perfect of grins.

Will approached Jeff, who was speaking with his assistant and his girlfriend. As much as he hated schmoozing, he'd learned over the years that if you didn't know when to step in and take your shot, opportunities would slip by like a missed subway on the B line.

"Hastings," Jeff said, raising his drink. "Glad you could make it out."

"My pleasure," Will said. He clinked his glass against Jeff's. "Happy birthday. Thanks for inviting us." He smiled and acknowledged the two women.

"Daphne, Elizabeth, do you mind giving Will and me a few minutes to chat?" Jeff said. He nodded toward an alcove on the other side of the room. "Let's go somewhere quiet," he said.

As they crossed the room, Will's gaze automatically landed on Maya, sitting alone at a table with her drink. He wanted to make this conversation quick—get through the business side of things and get back to her, where he belonged.

She looked stunning in her dress, and all he wanted was to spend the night at her side. Then return to their room, where there might be an act two to the incredible moment they'd just shared. It had almost killed him when he'd agreed that they needed to get dressed. They'd be back there soon, and he fully intended to show Maya again how drop-dead gorgeous he found her. How much he desired her.

But first, he had to close this deal.

"I'm sure you've heard I'm about to take a sizable gamble on this new franchise," Jeff said. "Have you read the books?"

"All four," Will said. "I loved them."

"What did you love about them?" Jeff asked, his eyes narrowing with curiosity. Will knew the question was more than just polite conversation—he was being tested.

"Timeless storytelling," Will said. "It appeals to everyone, no matter the age. Kids, grandparents—everyone in between. The celestial elements are awe-inspiring, but there's also a warning about the speed of human progress."

Jeff nodded.

"And those jetpacks... I mean, building those babies will be *fun*."

Jeff grinned. "Agreed. What's your instinct on casting?"

"I've heard good things about Michael Lawson," Will said. "I liked him in *Pirate's Eye*."

Jeff raised an eyebrow, intrigued. "Hmm," he said. "I've heard he's a bit of a diva on set."

"Nothing I can't handle," Will said.

"You did tame Oliver Marks."

"Took a few years off my life, but yeah," said Will, thinking back to the bad boy actor who'd slept with two of the female cast members a week apart, creating some challenging on-set dynamics. He'd also shown up to set under the influence more than once, still delivering a top-notch performance that made it challenging to reprimand him. "It's all about finding that balance—making them feel important but keeping them on their toes. The younger ones especially want to be treated like stars, but I know how to make them work for it."

They chatted for a few more minutes about the story, and Will could tell he was succeeding in what he was there to do.

"Let's go out and have a cigar, shall we?" Jeff said. "Continue this conversation outside."

Will bristled. He couldn't really say no. There was no verbal agreement yet. He glanced back at Maya, who was accepting another glass of champagne from a waiter. Hopefully she was okay for a few more minutes.

Half an hour passed, and Maya did her best to feign indifference that she was still sitting alone at a table.

She was relieved when Will finally appeared in the entrance to the restaurant with Jeff, then beelined it to her as Jeff turned to the bar.

"I'm sorry," he said, perching on the chair next to her. "You okay?"

"All good," she said, grateful to have him back by her side. "Just people watching. How did it go with Jeff?"

Will leaned over and kissed her on the cheek. "Pretty good, I think," he said in her ear, his rich voice setting off every alarm bell in her body. How long until they could be alone again together? "We're still chatting. I just wanted to check in with you."

Maya took a deep breath to temper the light annoyance that she was being left alone again. "How much longer do you think you'll be?" she asked.

"Give me ten more minutes," Will said. He fixed her in his deep gaze. "Then I'm all yours."

Maya nodded and watched as Will approached Jeff again, and the bartender passed them each a drink. She turned back to her own. She could manage ten more minutes.

A waiter came by and picked up Maya's empty glass. Had she already finished another drink? She offered Maya another cocktail from her tray, this one pale yellow with a single mint leaf floating in it.

Maybe it was the alcohol or the pure intoxicating feeling of being in this magical place with Will, but she definitely needed to slow down. She took a small sip of the cocktail, which was herbaceous and lemony and just the right amount of sweet. Maya sighed and forgot about her solitude for a moment. Everything on offer at this place was a little piece of heaven.

Her dreamlike state intensified when every now and then from the bar, Will locked eyes with her, giving the illusion that she was the only person in the room.

Twenty minutes later, Maya was still sitting alone at her table, watching the party play out in front of her. The awkwardness she'd felt earlier had completely dissipated, replaced by resentment. Guest after guest flocked to Will, shaking his hand and asking for photos together. He was clearly in his element in this room of tastemakers and people with influence.

She absent-mindedly took a few more sips of her drink, then checked her watch. How long was he going to be? Now she was more than annoyed. She decided to go to the bathroom, then she was going to march right over and stand by his side. Wasn't she his date, after all?

Maya stood up and immediately felt the effects of the alcohol. She focused on walking in a straight line to the lobby bathroom. Thank goodness for her flat Mary Jane shoes. It occurred to her as she navigated the room that she should eat something when she returned to the party.

When she returned to the dining room, an R&B artist had taken the mic, and couples were dancing in the middle of the room. Maya spotted Will next to the bar, deep in conversation with a beautiful woman who looked to be in her late thirties. Through her slightly blurry vision, she noticed that the woman was standing a bit too close for Maya's liking and was casually holding his arm and laughing as he apparently told her the funniest story in the world.

Emboldened by the wine—or was the last one a martini? She couldn't remember—Maya straightened her shoulders and waded through the crowd of partygoers over to where Will and the woman were talking. She was practically hanging off Will in her six-inch glossy black heels. Who did this woman think she was?

On her way, Maya grabbed a glass of white wine from a waiter's tray, taking a long sip as she approached. The woman was now saying something in Will's ear, and he looked up as Maya stopped right beside them.

Will flashed Maya a quick grin and slid his arm around her waist as though it was the most natural thing in the world. "Kendall, this is Maya," he said. She noticed he hadn't given her any other qualifier. "Maya, this is Kendall Hampton. She's the editor-in-chief of Flare Magazine."

Well, la di dah, thought Maya, taking another sip of her wine. The room was starting to swirl around her as she shook the woman's hand.

"We're doing a feature with Canadian artists wearing Canadian designers," Kendall said, smiling at Will. "I was just telling Will that he'd be amazing for the project."

I'll bet, thought Maya, nodding politely while picturing Kendall at a photo shoot with Will, fixing his collars and making bedroom eyes at him. Her pulse raced, thinking about how brazenly Will was allowing this woman to flirt with him. Clearly his interest in Maya being there with him was waning. Of course it was! She was just the flavor of the moment until he found another beautiful woman. She'd called it. This was what it would be like to date someone who existed in these circles.

"I'm—I'm going for a walk," Maya said, aware that her speech was slurring. She was—what had Lucas said?—*lit*.

"I'll come with you," Will said.

Kendall said nothing, but Maya could see by her expression that she was unimpressed.

"No, no, I'm just going to step outside for a moment. You stay here." Without waiting for a response, Maya turned and left, the whole room suddenly a blur, the music pulsing through the air and piling on more chaos to the thoughts and feelings rushing through her head.

The last thing she remembered after she spun around and marched away from Will and Kendall was Jeff's birthday cake being wheeled in through the door as she passed, a decadent multilayer chocolate cake all lit up with candles and sparklers. She couldn't help herself from reaching out and scooping a dollop of icing from the side of the cake, leaving a visible dent in the perfect buttercream, then popping it in her mouth.

Hers was better.

It took Maya a moment to remember where she was when she awoke in the morning. Her head was about to explode. She was sure of it. Any slight movement was dangerous. There was a nauseous turmoil rumbling in her stomach. Was it possible that the hotel was so close to the ocean that they were actually swaying in the waves, and she was not only hungover but also seasick? She rolled over and groaned.

Tentatively, she opened her eyes to the brightly lit area, with sun rays that seemed intent on making her hangover worse. How had she gotten back to the room? She pulled down the sheet and found she was still wearing her party dress. Was that icing on the skirt? Where was Will? She rolled over again to move closer to the bedside table, grabbed the bottle of water the hotel provided and finished half in four long gulps.

"You okay up there?" Will's voice came from the sitting area downstairs.

She squeezed her eyes shut. How badly had she embarrassed herself? How did she think she'd feel after having that many drinks, given that she only ever had one or two on a monthly basis?

"I'm okay," she croaked, slowly lifting herself into a sitting position. She felt for the floor, then stood up, the dizzying effects of the drinks still lingering. She padded to the bathroom, where she closed and locked the door and looked at herself in the mirror. Thank goodness she hadn't had to pass Will on the way.

She rooted around in Will's travel case and silently cheered when she located a bottle of ibuprofen. She shook two pills out in her hand, took some water and swallowed them. Hopefully they'd stay down. After lingering for a few restorative minutes in the shower, Maya wrapped herself in the soft terry cloth robe and tied her wet hair up in a bun. Far from perfect but definitely better.

She padded down the stairs to find Will with his feet up on the windowsill, fully dressed for the day in jeans and a Neil Young T-shirt, making some notes on his clipboard.

He sat up when he saw her and smiled. "Never seen someone wear a hangover so well," he said.

Maya blushed and rolled her eyes as she sank down in the armchair across from where he was sitting. "I'm really sorry," she said. "I'm so embarrassed."

Will stood up and brought her a tray from the desk on the other side of the room. "Don't be. It happens to the best of us." He flashed that perfect, effortlessly handsome smile, and Maya couldn't help but chastise herself for messing up what had been, up until that point, a great night. And now he was bringing her coffee. "Coffee and scones delivered this morning," he said, then checked his watch. "I can call down for more, though, if it's cold."

"What time is it?" she asked.

"It's just after ten," Will said. "We'll head to the airport in half an hour. Listen," he said. "I have to apologize. I shouldn't have left you alone for so long last night. It's just that Jeff was really wanting to get into detail about this new franchise, and—"

The memory of feeling like a solo partygoer surfaced and hit Maya with a pang of irritation. She waved her hand, doing her best to seem casual. "And everyone else was lined up to see you next," she said.

He flinched at her words. Maybe that was too sharp.

"Don't even think twice about it," she said, trying to sound casual. "You had a deal to make."

The truth was, she did feel slighted. Sure, she was disappointed that Will hadn't followed through on his promise to introduce her to anyone who might be interested in her work, but more, the connection she'd felt after they'd made love before the party felt so real, so strong... How had he been okay to just let her sit there like she was some kind of rent-a-date?

Through the haze of her hangover, she knew she'd been stupid to think that she and her little books had any business being in the mix at a party like that one. Or that Will saw her as any more than another small-town fling, a stop on the way to bigger, brighter things. She was way out of her league and, once again, had just been there to watch Will shine in his.

"I still shouldn't have done that," Will said, his voice quieter. "I feel bad."

Do you, though? she wanted to say. And did it really matter? It was time to go home, and she had no interest in drawing this out unnecessarily. "Did you make a deal?" she said instead, doing her best to sound chipper. The churning in her stomach wasn't helping. If there was any turbulence on the flight home, she'd be in trouble.

"It's looking good," Will said. "Although…" He paused. "It's a massive project. A few years' commitment. They're talking about shooting in the salt flats in Bolivia and the Atacama Desert. I'll be living in the middle of nowhere if I sign on."

"Well, that sounds amazing," Maya said, barely able to eke out the words at the thought of the scope of the project. There would be a multimillion-dollar budget and months of touring the world and walking red carpets following the shoot. All while she did her same walk to and from the bakery every morning and afternoon, made the same small talk with her regulars and sat in the same chair in her living room, staring at her laptop screen and imagining characters being swept off their feet in grand romantic gestures that were starting for the first time to feel completely unrealistic. "Congratulations."

Will nodded, but Maya noted that he'd lost the sparkle in his eye, and he didn't appear to be over the moon about the massive contract.

Whatever. He was clearly just trying to downplay it for her sake. Will Hastings, the number one student. Student council president, valedictorian. The pride of Sunset County. The Hollywood dynamo.

And here she was again, remembering what it was like to be in his shadow.

The drive back to the airport in the sleek black SUV, the sparkling interior of the jet's cabin on the flight home—something about the whole experience had lost the magic she'd felt on the way there, and she knew it wasn't just the hangover.

This fleeting fantasy, this silly dream of a world where she and Will could be something again—it was about time she woke up and let it go.

Chapter Twenty-One

Agatha helped Will get Gene to the car, and once his dad was settled in the front seat, Will closed the door. "Listen," he said to Agatha. "I can't tell you how much I appreciate how much you've helped my father. I know he could be a bit of a handful at times."

"Your father is a good man," Agatha said. "Never treated me with anything other than respect. We had some different opinions about some things, but he gave me a good chuckle now and then."

Will dug in his pocket and pulled out an envelope and passed it to the woman. "For your granddaughter," he said. "Or whatever else you want to do with it."

Agatha's eyes widened. "I couldn't possibly—"

"I insist," said Will. "It's the least I can do. Your job is a really important one, and I want to recognize you in some way."

"Thank you," Agatha said. Before he could move, Agatha was giving him a bone-cracking hug. Then she tapped on Gene's window and waved at him.

"My niece will look after you," she called as Will got into the driver side.

Will waved to Agatha, then started the car. "All set?" he asked Gene.

All Gene gave him was a grunt in return.

Will turned on the local radio station and allowed the banal quips of the radio hosts to fill the air as they drove to Gene's new home.

"Hey, why don't we stop by the bakery on the way and pick up one of those lemon Danishes you like?" Will said.

He hadn't heard from Maya since they'd returned from Aspen Cove. It had been a busy week out at the tree farm and then shooting outside the Briarwood, so there had been no reason to bump into Maya on Main Street. Still, he was starting to feel like the cold shoulder he'd felt the morning they'd returned to Sunset County wasn't a figment of his imagination or a product of Maya's hangover. He'd texted her later that day after Ivan had dropped her off at her place to see how she was feeling, but her response had been tepid and lacking interest in further conversation.

Gene didn't protest, so Will made a detour to Main Street and pulled up in front of the bakery.

"I'll be right back," said Will. He entered the bakery and was surprised to find a teenage boy sitting beside the counter, slouched in his seat and scrolling through his phone.

He sat straight up when Will came through the door, slipped his phone in his pocket and stood behind the cash. "Hi," the kid said. "What can I help you with today?"

The delivery was a bit awkward, but Will appreciated what seemed like a genuine attempt at customer service. "Just a lemon Danish," he said. He scanned the space behind Lucas, but it seemed like he was managing the bakery alone. "Is Maya around?"

"She's gone to the bank," Lucas said.

Will nodded. Maybe he could drop in again later. He was desperate to see Maya and know that things between them were okay. In some ways it felt pointless—he was leaving in a week. If anything, he should be welcoming the space between them, not trying to close it and make the inevitable more difficult.

But the logical side of his brain was taking a back seat to the memory of Maya's lips pressed against his, the soft trailing of her fingers on the skin of his back as they lay together, the light sigh of pleasure that escaped from her mouth when he'd kissed her naked skin, glowing in the honey hue of the setting sun.

"What's your name?" Will asked.

"Lucas," he said as he took a Danish out of the display case with a pair of tongs.

"How are you liking working at the bakery, Lucas?"

Lucas passed him the bag, then turned the payment console toward him. "I thought it would kind of suck. Like getting up early and everything. My mom made me get the job," he said, then pushed his hair out of his eyes and smiled a little. "But honestly, it's been cool."

"Every now and then our parents know what's good for us, I guess," Will said, suddenly recognizing the irony of the statement.

Lucas rolled his eyes. "Yeah. My mom. My guidance counselor. My soccer coach. Seems like everyone thinks they know what's best for me. *Go to university. Go to college. Study business. Study biology*," he mimicked in a sarcastic tone. He scoffed and shook his head. "Want a receipt?"

"No, thanks," said Will. He slid his wallet into his

back pocket. "So, if you don't mind me asking, what is it that you *want* to do?"

Lucas slumped back onto the stool with a sigh. "That's another question people keep asking me," he said. "I just don't have the answer to it. Like, I'm seventeen. And I'm supposed to have my whole life planned out?"

Poor kid. The weight of expectations was practically dripping off him. "Don't feel bad about taking some time to figure stuff out," Will said. "It'll come to you."

"Says you," Lucas asked, raising an eyebrow. "Aren't you that famous director? How many BMWs do you own?"

Will chuckled. "I guess some people might call me that. But to be honest, the way I was feeling when I was your age? Wasn't too far off from what you're going through."

"Oh yeah? So what'd you do?" It was clear Lucas was trying to sound indifferent, but Will could hear the curiosity in his voice.

"I did what I wanted to, regardless of what other people said. I followed my gut. No matter the noise around me."

"I guess you don't regret it?"

"I paid the price for it, in some ways," Will said. "My dad pretty much cut me off. I lost the most important person in my life, which, in retrospect, is my biggest regret. But at the end of the day, I trusted myself, and you'll never regret doing that."

Just then, the blare of a horn cut through the air. Will glanced out the window to see Gene glaring at him from the car. "Speaking of my dad…thanks for the chat. Good luck with everything."

Lucas gave a slight nod. "Hope some of that BMW energy rubs off of me," he said.

Will chuckled to himself as he exited the bakery.

Teenagers.

Maya leaned against the fridge in the back of the bakery, tucked away from the sightline of the front room, clutching the cash float she'd just picked up from the bank with her eyes closed, breathing deeply.

Just the sound of Will's voice wafting through from the front of the bakery was enough to undo her. And hearing his words was pushing her to the brink.

Ever since she'd stepped out of the production van that had driven them home from the airport and bid Will what she knew was a lukewarm goodbye at best, she'd felt sick to her stomach. Not even an extended cuddle session with Bruce was enough to pull her out of her funk.

She'd completely fallen for Will again. And being by his side on that trip, then the perfection of making love to him again had dug her deep into that hole.

Now, hearing his conversation with Lucas, she was overtaken by confusion.

He'd broken her heart, yes, but maybe eighteen-year-old Will hadn't really seen another option. She'd spent so much time feeling woe-is-me, and rightfully so, but had she ever really imagined how much it had hurt for him to be so rejected by his father? The weight of another kind of pressure, the pressure of expectation? And had she added to that, with her naive insistence on maintaining the perfection of their relationship, in a situation where it was going to be impossible to do so?

I lost the most important person in my life, his words echoed in her mind. *My biggest regret.*

But that was years ago, what realistically amounted to a teenage fling, and here they were. They'd grown too far apart, with lives undeniably too different. Life had happened. *And, and, and...*

Maya reached for what was after *and*, but she was out of excuses. The problem was, she had no clue what to do next.

She gathered herself, then entered the front of the bakery where Lucas was wiping the counter with a wet rag. "All good here?" she asked, with a casual ease she hoped was hiding the swirling thoughts in her mind.

She opened the cash register and set about sorting the bills and change into the correct spots, ready for the few remaining Sunset County residents who still traded in cash.

"All good," Lucas said. "We're running low on cheddar scones, though."

"They're always popular on Saturdays," said Maya. She stood for a moment, watching as he carefully wiped the corners between the counter and the display case, not letting a single crumb escape his cloth.

Lucas might be a teacher's worst nightmare. His lack of direction no doubt kept Cassie awake at night. And with those high cheekbones and dark lashes he was going to break more than a few hearts in his early adult life. But the truth was, he was shaping up to be an excellent employee.

"Go flip the sign in the window," Maya said, nodding toward the entrance. "In the next thirty minutes,

I'm going to teach you the art of the cheddar scone. And you will carry this skill with you your entire life."

Lucas dropped the towel on the counter and grinned. "Really?" he said. "Sick."

"Really," said Maya. "The secret, as always, is butter."

Pinecrest Haven was situated across the street from the local elementary school. Will imagined it must be nice for the residents to hear the playful shrieks and laughter coming from the playground at recess and lunch breaks, and they were likely treated to some performances and Valentine's Day card activities.

There was a nice garden planted out front, and lots of windows. It wasn't anything fancy, but it was homey and well maintained and would allow Gene to stay in the town he'd lived in his entire life.

Will pulled the car into a spot close to the entrance. They'd go inside first and get instructions for where to bring all of Gene's belongings.

He got out and jogged to the other side of the car to help Gene, but Gene waved away his hand and slowly got himself to standing.

Will followed his father up the path. He was dragging his feet a bit, but at least he was walking into the building willingly.

A young woman with dark curly hair and purple scrubs greeted them in the entrance, holding a clipboard and grinning widely. "You must be Mr. Hastings!" she said, her voice warm and optimistic.

Well cast, thought Will. Her sunny disposition likely had a big part to play in why management put her in her role, the welcoming committee for people entering what would likely be their final home.

Gene glared at her and waved his hand as though he could wipe her out of the picture.

"I'm Jessica," she said, the smile still hanging on. "I'm here to welcome you and get you settled in your room today!" She looked at Will. "And you're Mr. Hasting's son? We've spoken on the phone. Will, right?"

"Nice to meet you," said Will, extending his hand. "I've got some things in the car to bring in. But maybe you can show us the space first?"

"Follow me," said Jessica.

Will started to move in the same direction as Jessica but noticed Gene staring at the bookshelves lining the entrance, with chairs positioned around them.

"Not even one single James Patterson," he said. "What the hell kind of library is this?"

Will took his father's arm and nudged him gently. "Come on, Dad. I'll get you any book you want once we're all settled."

Gene mumbled something under his breath about it not being bright enough but shuffled his feet and allowed Will to lead him.

Will's phone buzzed in his pocket. He slid it out to find a message from Maya. How's it going there? He paused before replying.

Well, I wouldn't say he's reveling in his dream home, Will typed. Not enough James Patterson. And apparently it isn't bright enough. He added a shrugging emoji to the end of the text and hit Send.

He scanned the room, which was warm and quiet. There was a double hospital bed set up in the corner, and in the small living space, a couch faced a television mounted to the wall. A sitting chair had a view of both the television and the window, which looked out to a pretty courtyard with a garden in the middle where benches and bistro tables with umbrellas were arranged. It was clean and nice, but Will reminded himself that Gene would find fault with any setup.

Over the next half hour, Jessica explained the features of the home, noting different activities and schedules, which she also posted to the back of Gene's door.

"Do you need to use the washroom, Dad?" Will asked.

"I want to see where I'll be eating," Gene said. "You do have food here, right?"

Jessica smiled again, exuding the patience of a saint. "Of course, Mr. Hastings. I think you'll love the meals. Our chefs do a great job. In fact," she said, checking her watch, "it's just about lunchtime! Why don't you follow me down to the dining hall? And, Will, you're welcome to stay for lunch, too."

"Sounds great," said Will. He glanced at his father, whose stony expression hadn't changed.

They walked with Jessica down the hallway, passing some other residents: an older woman with a walker and a man being pushed in a wheelchair by a nurse. They both nodded their heads politely as they passed, but Gene continued to stare straight ahead, not even reacting when Jessica announced that the special of the day was roast beef, which was Gene's favorite.

"That's a good sign to me," Will said as he settled in across the table from Gene.

"This is Jerry," Jessica said, as a middle-aged man

wearing an apron approached the table with some laminated menus. "He'll be serving you today."

"I'm not hungry," said Gene.

"Why don't you order something?" Will said. "Maybe you'll be hungry by the time it comes."

Gene slammed a fist down on the table. "Goddammit, I'm not hungry," he said.

A few of the other residents seated at nearby tables were making no secret of the fact that they were checking out the new member of their community, who, it was clear, had no interest in a pleasant dining experience.

"Why don't I bring you some bread," said Jerry, "and you can take a few minutes to think about it?"

"Thank you," said Will, and Jerry moved to the next table, where three ladies wearing lipstick and three shades of pink were assembled.

"Dad," said Will quietly. "I know this isn't your number one choice—"

"You're damn right it's not," he said. He glared at Will. "You've got a lot of nerve coming out here, after all this time, taking me out of my home against my will. Now you're going to sell it and keep the profits. I should have known you were out to get me."

Will paused. "Dad, this has nothing to do with money," he said. "I can assure you I have plenty of money and don't need yours."

"Show off," Gene muttered.

The waiter returned with a basket of bread and a plate with foil-wrapped butter packets. "Here you are," he said. "Any interest in anything off the menu?"

"Where's the margarine?" Gene said, looking up at Jerry with disdain.

"Uh, we actually only have butter, sir," Jerry said.

"Bull," said Gene. "This whole place is bull."

"Dad, come on, just—"

"We can arrange for some margarine for Mr. Hastings, can't we, Jerry?" a voice came from over Will's shoulder.

He turned to see Maya, her arms piled with books and a shopping bag hanging from her elbow. Her cardigan had strawberries embroidered on it, and her hair hung loose and wavy around her face, which Will noted, seemed to look prettier every time he saw her. Just the sight of her sent a flutter through his chest, lifting his spirits in a way no one else could.

She approached Gene and placed both hands on his shoulders. "Although I have to tell you, Mr. Hastings, you'd be much better off eating butter. For the taste and for your health."

Gene's expression softened, and the corner of his mouth seemed to be fighting the slightest of grins. "I like margarine," he said.

Maya looked at Jerry. "Then we can get margarine, right? That can't be too hard. What if I drop it off myself at the end of every week?"

"I mean, if you want to supply it, I can't see management having much of a problem with that," Jerry said.

"Problem solved," said Maya, grinning. She glanced up at Will and winked.

"Thank you," he mouthed. He cleared his throat. "We were just having a look at the menu, but I think maybe we'll wait for dinner to eat, right, Dad?"

"I'm not hungry," Gene repeated. He looked at Maya, whose arms were still overloaded. "What's all that?"

"Oh, just a few things for your room," she said. "Can I see your new digs?"

"You mean my prison?" Gene said.

Will bristled. "Dad, for god's sake, you—"

"Let's go make it into a real home, shall we?" Maya said, extending her hand for Gene to grab onto while balancing the bags in her arms. He allowed her to assist him and kept hold of her elbow. He started to walk, then it became clear he wasn't sure where he was going.

"Out that door, then right," Will said. "Last door on the left at the end of the hallway."

Maya led Gene out, while Will trailed behind with Jessica. He looked at the plate that Jerry was just delivering to one of the other tables. The roast beef didn't look half bad. Gene would be fine.

"Part of our work for the next week is to help your father learn his way around the place," said Jessica.

To what end? thought Will. It seemed like Gene could barely keep information in his head for one minute, never mind learn the layout of a whole new building.

Jessica must have read his mind. "The mind is a funny thing," she said. "You might notice your dad still remembering minute details of things that happened years earlier, but forget what he was talking about twenty seconds ago. We'll keep his mind as sharp as possible by exposing him to novel situations and asking him to keep learning."

Will nodded, then stopped in the entrance to his father's room and watched while Maya helped Gene lower himself into the easy chair.

She pulled a stack of books from the bag and set them on the coffee table in front of him. "Here are the three latest Pattersons. One of them is a collaboration with

Michael Crichton. Not usually my thing, but it looks kind of good."

Without waiting for Gene to say anything, Maya pulled a small lamp from her bag and placed it on the table beside the couch. Will watched as she fiddled with the cord, flicked a switch, and a moment later, the already bright space was a few shades brighter.

"That better, Mr. Hastings?" she asked, flashing him an irresistible smile.

"Bit better, thanks, dear," Gene said, his voice low and gravelly.

"One more thing," said Maya. She dug down to the bottom of the bag and pulled out the old Elvis clock from the kitchen. Will watched as Gene struggled to contain his delight. "We'll need maintenance to come by with a hammer and nail," Maya said. "But I thought this might make it feel a little more like home here."

A rush of adoration washed over Will. Maya always made everything better. Not only that, he was beginning to realize that had he made a little more effort with Gene, maybe things could have been a bit better between them. Not perfect. But better.

"Looks like you've got lots of people looking out for you," Jessica said. She turned to Will. "I'll see if someone from maintenance can come by, and I'll let you help your father get settled. If you need any help moving in boxes, just let me know, and one of us can give you a hand."

"Appreciate it," said Will, and then they were three. Will, his father and the woman who was brightening up a challenging day more than any lamp ever could.

"That was nice of Maya, wasn't it, Dad?" Will said. He took a seat on the couch and picked up one of the hardcover books, turning it over in his hand. How long would his dad be able to read? To follow a plot without having to go back several pages? Worse, not recognizing the words on the page?

When he glanced up, he found Maya adjusting the level of a framed print of Monet's *Water Lilies*. She moved it just so, then stood back and edged it just a little bit farther.

For a split second, Will was so struck by her quiet determination to make things pleasant for his father that he almost couldn't breathe.

So when his father spoke—"I hate that goddamn painting. There are other nice paintings in the world. Why the hell is that one plastered over every wall in the world?"—Will felt a strange sense of relief. At least his father's sharp tongue was still there, cutting through the tension of the moment.

Maya swirled around, a look of mock indignation on her face. "But, Mr. Hastings, the water lilies are so serene! What do you want? Some kind of battlefield reenactment or something?" She considered. "I mean it's not my thing, but I'm sure I could find it for you."

His father scowled, leaning back in his chair. "What I want is to be back in my living room," he muttered. "Where I can look out the window at something worth looking at." Then, his voice shifted, softer but with a touch of frustration. "And where's Leon?"

Maya looked at Will. "Leon?" she said. "You mean—"

Will bristled. "Our cat," he said, giving her a look he hoped she could interpret. "We'll bring Leon over later, Dad," he added, his voice more even than he felt.

He could feel Maya's eyes on him, searching his expression, but he avoided her gaze. He knew he shouldn't lie. But it was easier in the moment. It felt like the thing he needed to do to keep the fragile balance of the room intact.

"Dad, I'm going to get some stuff from the car," he said. "I'll be right back."

"I'll help," said Maya.

"No, no, I'm fine," Will said. If anything, Maya had a calming effect on his father. He was filled with gratitude that she'd shown up like she did, before Gene caused a meltdown that would get him kicked out of the facility before he even had a chance to settle in. "I'll be right back."

Will left Maya and Gene in his room and exited to the parking lot to grab the suitcase and last box of Gene's belongings. Just as he got to the car, he felt his phone vibrating in his pocket.

His executive producer's name was on the screen. That wasn't good. At this juncture in the project, their involvement was usually minimal. Hopefully nothing had happened to any of the cast or crew.

"Will speaking," he said.

"Hey, Will, it's Laura Morris."

"Everything okay?" Will said.

"No need to be concerned. Do you have a second?"

He didn't want to leave Maya for too long with his dad, but something told him he needed to take this call. "Uh, yeah, what's up?"

"We need to talk about the next few days," Laura said. "With the two half days we missed with Cam going to the hospital, then the incident with the dogs and the budget overage for changing locations—"

"Which was completely worth it," Will said firmly.

"I don't doubt it. But the final scene is just way too expensive. We need to come up with a different ending."

"That's in five days," said Will, mentally scanning the schedule for the week. "Are you kidding me?" He thought about the mountains they'd have to move to come up with a whole different ending. Not only would there be rewrites, but they'd need location permits. New wardrobe. Storyboards and shot lists. Blocking and rehearsals and set design.

"I know you're used to...bigger budget projects," Laura said. "But in our world, we just kind of roll with these things."

"What about the contingency budget?"

The other side of the line was quiet. "You ate it up."

"I ate it up?"

"Your salary," Laura said. "You're expensive."

"I did take a pay cut," Will said. He squeezed his eyes shut with the recognition that he wasn't going to win this battle. "All right, I'll get the team together tonight."

"Let us know when you have a loose plan, and if there's anything we can do."

"Will do," he said. He tapped the screen to end the call. "Dammit," he muttered. He texted Shauna. Emergency meeting in an hour, he wrote.

A text buzzed again right away, but it wasn't from Shauna. It was from Hayley. Two offers have come in this morning! A foreign buyer and a local—neither has seen the site but both offers look good. Call me.

Will took in a slow, steadying breath. This definitely wasn't the time to go back inside and tell Gene that news. He had a production to save.

And in the meantime, he had boxes to move.

***

Twenty minutes later, all of Gene's belongings were moved into his room, and Maya and Will were making quick work of organizing everything while Gene napped in his chair.

"Thank you again for doing this," Will said quietly as Maya hung the last sweater in the closet. "You really didn't have to."

"I wanted to," said Maya. "Is there anything else at the house I can help bring over?"

"There are a couple things, but I have to get to a meeting," he said. He paused. Was now the right time to tell Maya about the change of plans for the movie's ending?

Having her there felt nice. Like a partnership. There was no trace left of the coolness he'd felt the last time they'd been together. Revealing the bump in the plans felt like it might disrupt what, until now, was a really nice day. But then again, if she found out about it from someone else, he'd have hell to pay.

"Listen, I'm going to wake my dad up to say bye and then let Jessica know we're leaving and that I'll be back later tonight. Can I talk to you before we leave, though?"

"Of course," said Maya. "I'll meet you outside."

Maya left Will with his father, then exited to the sunny front entrance of the lodge, which was decorated with pumpkins and cornstalks and a cheery scarecrow.

She took a deep breath of the crisp fall air, a rush of something unmistakable running through her. In spite of the nagging feeling that she and Will lived in opposite worlds, there was no denying that she'd completely fallen for Will again, and this time it felt different. Of course, they were adults now. But unlike the first day Will had arrived in town, she found herself trusting him. Maybe in another life, things would have gone differently. Was it wrong, though, to dip a toe into this thing, whatever it was? Just to see?

"Thanks for waiting," Will said. His expression was drawn.

"Everything okay?"

"He just told me I could go to hell, so…" He paused, and she could tell he was forcing a smile. "So yeah."

Maya felt a pang of sympathy. "I'm sorry," she said. "Do you think—are you going to try to patch things up with him before you leave town?"

Will rolled his eyes and ran his hand through his hair. "I think we both know that's a fool's errand," he said, then looked away.

She hated seeing him so defeated. Gene was a challenging character, but surely they could come to some sort of peace before Will left town again. Who knew how quickly Gene's health would deteriorate? "I think you're going to have to make the move," Maya said, trying to be gentle.

"I'm not sure how much more I can do than what I'm doing," he said, gesturing to the lodge. "He hasn't even uttered so much as thank-you."

"I'm sure it's hard for him," Maya said. "Knowing he's not getting better. And having to move away from the place he's lived in for his entire life."

Will shook his head, then exhaled. "It sucks. I get it. I just wish he didn't have to be such a pain in the ass."

Maya paused. "I really do think that if you told him

how you feel, you might get some kind of resolution. Before it's too late."

Will's expression darkened. "I know you think everything in life will magically turn out *happily ever after*. But that's not real life, Maya. Real life is, let's face it, awful sometimes. My dad is sick. He's also not going to all of a sudden become the loving and supportive father I've wanted my whole life." Will's voice rose, growing more frayed with every word.

Maya wanted to shift gears, her instinct to calm him bubbling up, but she couldn't help what came out of her mouth next. "It could be happy if you just made the decision to make it so," she said. "You have a way of deciding things won't work out before you've even tried."

Will's expression shifted from exasperation to incredulity. "You have no idea," he said, his voice tight with something darker now.

"I'm sorry," Maya said. "I just—"

"You just always have to butt in," he cut her off sharply and shook his head, then looked at his watch. "I've got more important things to deal with than your advice. Everything's falling apart. My dad, the production." He let out a breath like he was about to explode. "The film's budget is running out, and we have to figure out a new ending that doesn't cost so much. So here I am! Trying to make things better. I just know where it matters to focus my energy."

Maya took a sharp breath in, her stomach twisting. "What? What do you mean, they're changing the ending?"

He didn't look at her. Instead, Will unlocked his car

door and slid in. "Honestly, Maya, just let me do my job." His voice was cold now, all edge.

Before she could say another word, he slammed his door shut, and his engine roared to life. He disappeared from the parking lot, leaving her standing there, hollowed out by his words.

Chapter Twenty-Two

There was no world in which Maya would ever regret the moment she walked into the Sunset County Animal Shelter the day she adopted Bruce. It might have seemed impulsive at the time, but she had to chalk it up to instinct. Because now, sitting on her couch with him nestled against her chest, breathing quietly and every so often gently licking her hand as she stroked his fur, the idea of Bruce not being in her world was an impossibility.

The moment she'd returned home from Pinecrest Haven, flung her purse on the kitchen table, then dove onto the couch, pulling the quilt her mother had made her over her head, Bruce had transformed from the rambunctious, wriggling, yappy attention-seeker to something better than any therapy session could ever be.

"I love you," she whispered, breathing in the puppy scent of his fur. Her eyes welled up with tears, and she pulled him in even closer.

Try as she might, and as sweet as Bruce was being, she couldn't erase the look on Will's face and the tone of his voice from her mind.

She shouldn't have pushed.

But Will needed to be pushed.

And she didn't want to be selfish and make it all about

her, but hello! He decided to drop the major detail that he was on his way to brainstorm a new ending like he needed to make it to the grocery store to pick up toilet paper before it closed?

Through her tears, her jaw clenched. This whole thing was turning out to be a complete disaster, and it was all because she'd done exactly what Valerie had told her not to do: get her hopes up.

Will's words rang in her mind. *You think everything in life will magically turn out happily ever after.*

What the hell was wrong with being optimistic?

The final scene of her movie played in her mind, but suddenly, it was all in black and white, not the vibrant technicolor it had played in when she'd written it.

Now it was in the hands of someone who clearly didn't believe in even the possibility of a happy ending.

She wasn't sure what disappointed her more. The idea that her story was no longer going to translate perfectly to film or the reality that while she'd thought Will might have evolved and changed, and that maybe, just maybe, there had been a glimmer of a chance for them to try again, he hadn't changed one single bit.

Will stared out the window of his room at the Briarwood, watching as a young couple paddled a yellow canoe close to the shore. The trees reflected their vibrant colors in the water, which sparkled in the early evening sun. Easy. Serene.

Unlike the panic brewing in his stomach. He was set to meet with Shauna and the rest of his team in twenty minutes and wanted to bring a few creative ideas to the table, to justify his salary and back up his experience.

But all he could think about was the look of disappointment and rejection in Maya's eyes when he allowed himself a brief glimpse back at her when he peeled out of the parking lot.

Now, not only was he feeling like a complete jerk, but he couldn't summon any kind of creative solution to this problem they were facing.

As much as he'd made fun of the ski slope proposal, the more he thought about it, it really was the perfect ending. Sarah loved grand gestures and Ben liked to play life on the safer side, so the fast-paced athletic feat showed his growth as a character, and Sarah getting stuck on a chairlift gave him time to confess his undying love.

He closed his eyes, trying to think of something to replace it. "Come on," he muttered. Holiday magic. Hot chocolate bomb with a ring inside? Meh. A ring around a reindeer's antler? No. No more animals. A bent knee at midnight in front of the tree in the town square? Ugh. These movies got away with some element of contrivance, but he wasn't about to go that far.

A light rapping sounded at his door. "Will?" Shauna's voice called. "We're all downstairs."

He took a deep breath and gathered his notebook. "Coming," he said.

An hour later, the team was still throwing around ideas, but nothing was sticking. He could tell they were getting frustrated with each idea he shot down. They were fine, he supposed. But nothing felt right. And he'd had enough experience to know that if you didn't stick the landing, no matter how good the rest of the film was, ultimately it would be tainted by an unsatisfying conclusion.

"Maybe we can just stick with the ski scene, but without snow," Shauna said. "I mean, green Christmases are more of a thing these days, aren't they?"

"Mountain biking instead of skiing?" said Cam, leaning back in his chair. "Rad. I can get on board with that."

Will raised an eyebrow. "Keep your thinking caps on, folks, and if anyone has a brilliant idea, text me. We need a plan in place by tomorrow night." He stood up and picked up his things, trying to project the air of a confident leader and mask the brewing panic he was feeling. "I'll be in my room if anyone needs me."

Will scaled the stairs, tossed his clipboard on the table, then flopped backward on his bed, mind swirling.

This was ridiculous. He was an Academy award nominee. *New York Magazine* had called him a visionary on the brink of reinventing a new era of classic American cinema. And here he was, completely incapable of figuring out an ending for a movie about a ski resort wedding. This was bad.

No amount of pacing around his room, standing under the extremely hot, then extremely cold, then extremely hot again shower, even scrolling through Pinterest (that was a new one) was doing the trick. So five minutes after midnight, Will crawled into bed, the wakeup call in just under six hours looming like a brewing storm.

He was frustrated. Defeated. Disappointed in himself.

But after lying in bed staring at the ceiling for an hour, it was confirmed. What he wasn't was tired.

He knew what he needed to do. Whenever he got caught in a rut, the best place to be was back on set, as close as possible to being in the world of the story, where the possibility of inspiration felt more tangible.

Will pulled on a pair of jeans and a crew neck sweatshirt, grabbed his jacket and keys and clipboard and quietly let himself out the front of the inn into the inky black night. Aside from a gentle breeze blowing a small pile of leaves on the ground on the path to the parking lot, the night was still and deserted.

Ten minutes later, he pulled into a spot at the end of Main Street in front of the production office.

Downtown Sunset County looked completely different now, deserted, not buzzing with the same energy of every other day he'd been there.

He pocketed his keys, then checked the passcode for the door on his phone and keyed it in on the lock pad.

The room was dark and quiet. Lights blinked along the wall where batteries were plugged in to charge, and the main camera sat on a tripod. He approached it and flipped out the screen that would allow him to screen some of the footage from the past several days.

He scrolled through the clips, nodding in satisfaction at the shot compositions. The snow, especially, looked perfect. Worth every cent.

When he got to the bakery scene, he tapped Play and watched as Maya handed over the cookies to Ginger and Blake. The warmth of her expression, the way she filled the shot with sunshine, almost made him feel the glow through the screen. She was radiant. Beautiful. Magnetic. Everything he'd always known…but it meant something different now. Something sharper.

He felt a lump in his throat, knowing that he was the one who wasn't managing to make her dream come true.

Part of him was tempted to finance the ending scene himself, but he knew that would push Maya even farther away. His wealth, his world... It all seemed to make her feel less than.

Even though she was everything,

A light rapping on the glass of the door made him almost jump out of his skin. He jammed a few buttons on the camera until the video stopped playing, then stood for a moment. Who would be up at this hour?

The knock sounded again "Will?" he heard from the other side of the door. The voice was faint, but he had no doubt who it was.

Maya.

He flicked the lock and swung open the door, and there she was, clutching her coat around her shoulders with one hand and holding Bruce's leash with the other. Her hair was in a messy bun atop her head, stray wisps falling loosely around her face. Her sparkling green eyes were tired, but he'd never seen a sight more beautiful in his life.

"Maya," he said. "What are you doing here?"

"I couldn't sleep," she said. "So I thought I would just start early at the bakery. I've been wanting to work on my cannelloni recipe lately, so..." She glanced past him, her gaze flicking to the chaos behind him, which looked partly like a production office and partly like a department store at Christmas, with all the trees still set up and decorated, waiting to be used as background items. "Then I saw the light on here. Late night production meeting for one?" she asked.

"I couldn't sleep, either," said Will. "This ending is

driving me crazy, and I just thought being here might..." He paused, surveying her expression. "What?"

Maya's eyes flickered for a moment, then she looked like she was barely holding it together. A tightness gripped his chest. She seemed like she was on the verge of tears, and that was one thing he couldn't handle right now. She moved past him and went to the tree, turning over one of the ornaments in her hand.

He stood, frozen, unsure. What he wanted was to gather her in his arms, kiss her on the forehead and stroke the soft strands of hair away from her face. But he sensed that might not be what she needed.

"I'm sorry," he said, the words tumbling out in a rush. "I know you were really disappointed that things weren't going to turn out as planned. I—" He stopped and joined her by the tree.

Maya reached out, placed her hand on his arm and searched his expression. "You actually care," she said quietly. Her eyes welled up with tears, but she shook her head and bit her lip slightly, then blinked them away.

Her words hit him in the heart. "Of course I care," he said. He reached out to grab her hand in his and fixed her in his gaze. "You have no idea how much."

For a moment, Maya didn't respond. She looked away, shaking her head as if trying to push the feelings down. Her breath left her in a frustrated sigh.

"I don't get it," she said, her voice quieter now but no less intense. "The past couple of weeks, you've made me feel like this is the last place in the world you wanted to be, like this project was the last thing you wanted to work on. It's hard to believe that you've suddenly...turned a corner." She shook her head, her voice trailing off in confusion and hurt. "I just don't understand."

"I'll admit, I wasn't exactly sold on the idea," Will said, his voice low. "And with everything going on... honestly, I wasn't feeling too good about anything. But being with you, seeing this all through your eyes..." He stopped, weighing his words carefully. "You set the stage for something really beautiful, you know. I just wish I could've done a better job of helping to bring it to life."

Maya blinked again, then turned her head to the side as she wiped the corner of her eye. "You don't have to apologize," she said. "I was too hard on you. My expectations were too high, and I didn't give you any reason to believe I trusted you to do right by this thing. But the truth is..." She paused and took a deep, steadying breath. "The truth is I was afraid you were going to outshine me again. The way you always used to."

"I don't even know what—"

"You were always so smart, everything came easy to you. And look at you, a success. Everything figured out... It made me feel small. And that's my own fault, not yours."

Will took a step toward her and took her hand in his. "If there's anything I know in this world, it's that you own every room you walk into. It's like you're glowing or something, you light up every space you're in. You have a gift. You're anything but small."

Maya looked up at him. The space between them closed as she closed her eyes and tilted up her chin, and he met her lips in a soft, perfect kiss.

He pulled back slightly and took something out of his pocket and pressed it in her hand.

"What's this?" she said. She raised her palm, examining the little figurine.

"You were right," he said quietly. "There's something missing on the tree."

She looked up at him, her eyes sparkling with curiosity. "What do you mean?" He watched as recognition flooded her expression. "Is this...?" she said.

"You're right," he repeated, watching her read the sparkly gold star card she'd given him all those years ago before he left town. He'd kept in his pocket since they'd returned from Aspen Cove, thinking it might make him feel closer to her. "A tree—"

"Isn't a tree without a star," Maya finished. She smiled, and the sight of it lit him up from head to toe.

He gestured toward the tree. "Want to do the honors?"

"But wait," she whispered. "Won't this screw with—what's it called again—continuation?"

"Continuity," Will said, lowering his voice to match hers. "I won't tell if you won't. It'll be our own little Easter egg in the movie."

She grinned, clearly delighted. "I love that. Very much." She stepped toward the tree, glancing over her shoulder. "I guess I should put it somewhere inconspicuous."

Will raised an eyebrow, unable to stop his grin from spreading. "There's nothing inconspicuous about you. Put it wherever you want."

He watched as she placed the ornament carefully toward the top of the tree, then stepped back to admire it. "There," she said. "Now it's perfect."

"I couldn't agree more," he said. He took her hand in his, and by the light of the now perfect tree, he dipped his head down and kissed her. It was every bit a kiss straight out of the movies, and he felt the real magic in every cell of his body.

Outside under the streetlights, Will locked up the office, then turned to Maya. "You're not really going to bake at this hour, are you?" he asked. "Let me drive you home."

"We still haven't figured out the perfect ending," she said.

We, he thought. *Of course.* "I don't know why I've been banging my head against the wall," he said. "I should have asked you in the first place."

Maya yawned and clapped her hand over her mouth. "Sorry," she said. "I actually don't know how much use I'm going to be tonight."

"Tomorrow, after the shoot," he said. The idea of waiting until the last minute was still a bit gut churning, but he felt a whole lot more confident knowing he'd get Maya's input. "Working dinner?"

Maya paused, searching his face. "Sounds great," she said finally. "Just don't forget, my bedtime is a lot earlier than yours."

"I'll make sure the shoot day is efficient," he said. "Let me drive you two home."

"Bruce would never say no to VIP service," Maya said, grinning.

Will took Maya's hand in his and kissed her again under the dim glow of the streetlight. "I can't wait to take you out tomorrow night," he murmured quietly in her ear.

Maya looked up, her eyes sparkling. "I can't wait to dress up for you again," she whispered back.

***

Will drove himself to set the next morning and arrived to the usual flurry of activity. Even though this was a very different type of movie than he was used to directing, the life cycle of a film shoot remained the same. It started with mild chaos, then settled into a comfortable working pace. Too bad this one would be over in a matter of days.

When he approached the production office to check in on Ginger and Blake, the sound of cheering came from inside. He found Shauna, Skylar, Cam and Stu gathered around the camera, watching something on screen.

Shauna turned to him, her eyes wide. "Here he is!" The others looked up. "You did it! This is amazing!"

Will stopped in his tracks when his gaze landed on the screen and a paused image of him and Maya standing in front of the tree. "Oh no," he muttered. In his haste to turn off the camera when Maya had knocked the night before, he must have hit Record. And every last bit of their conversation was now entertainment for the entire crew?

"I love that you two ran the scene. With blocking and props and everything!" Shauna said. "There was a part where you were both whispering, and we couldn't make out the lines, so you'll have to fill us in. I mean, obviously we'll need to shoot some other angles, close-ups and everything. But could there be a better ending? That gold star, that harkens back to the nighttime scene, when Ben says it's stupid to wish on stars, but now he's finally come around? They're going to work together to save the wedding? It's just…perfect!"

"Having the whole wedding production on screen was

totally unnecessary," Skylar said. "We just need Sarah and Ben. Alone together. Settling their differences. The fact that it's at the location of their original conflict is so good."

"Agreed," Stu piped up. He sniffled and pulled a tissue from his pocket. "It's beautiful in its simplicity."

Will was speechless as he digested what Shauna was saying. His conversation with Maya played out in his mind. It...it really was perfect. It was real and heartfelt. And Sarah and Ben really did need each other and one another's complementary strengths. No ski lifts or fake snow required.

The rest of the movie flashed through his mind, and suddenly the credits were rolling.

He did his best to keep his cool and cleared his throat. "Get production on it," he said. "We'll be ready to shoot Friday."

"On it," said Shauna. She leaned in. "And Will," she said, a mischievous glint in her eye. "I didn't know you were such a good actor. That kiss looked...pretty realistic."

Will hoped Shauna didn't notice his cheeks going fifteen shades of red. "Ginger and Blake don't need any coaching from me, that's for sure," he said. "All right, let's get on with the day."

Shauna glanced at her watch. "We'll be ready to roll in half an hour."

Perfect, thought Will. "I'll be around."

He slipped out the back door and walked behind the Main Street businesses until he could smell the scent of sugar and cinnamon. The back door to Flour Child was propped open, the sounds of pop music floating from the space.

***

As a rule, Maya didn't lick her spoons or spatulas or any other kitchen tool that got coated with batter or melted chocolate or tasty crumbly bits. It was tempting, but she saved her calories for the always superior final products.

But this morning felt like a morning to indulge. So she picked up the spoon she'd been using to drizzle white chocolate on top of the pumpkin spice scones and popped the whole thing in her mouth, letting the sweet velvety goodness melt over her tongue. "Mmm," she murmured.

The only thing she'd have chosen over the white chocolate was Will's lips on hers again. She took a deep breath in, remembering the perfect warmth of his kiss, of the moment. She let out another satisfied moan just as the air in the room shifted and cooled.

She opened her eyes to find Will poking his head through the doorway, a sly grin tugging at the edges of his lips. "Looks like I'm walking into a Meg Ryan at Katz's Deli moment," he said.

She tossed the spoon in his direction, far enough away to avoid hitting him but close enough to get him to duck as the spoon hit the wall and clanged to the floor. "Can't a girl eat some breakfast white chocolate in peace?"

"Is that what that was?" Will said, stepping into the kitchen, his eyes sparkling with amusement. "What's on the menu tomorrow? I'll be back to watch."

"Get out of here," Maya said. The truth was, she couldn't have been happier to see him standing in the doorway.

Will glanced over the racks of pastries cooling on the

counter. "You've been busy," he said, his voice a mix of admiration and amusement.

"Just trying to stay awake," Maya said. She paused. "I had a hard time getting back to sleep when I got home."

"Is that right?" Will said playfully. "Thinking about the ending again?"

She took a deep breath as he drew nearer, her heart beating a little faster, and shook her head slowly. "No. You?"

"Tried to. But I had...other things on my mind."

"I see," said Maya. "That was some kiss."

"About that kiss," Will said, a mischievous glint in his eyes, "it might have just earned us a celebratory dinner tonight instead of a working one."

Maya's eyes widened. "What do you mean?" she asked, leaning in slightly, eager for whatever twist he had in mind.

Will scratched his neck. "I accidentally hit the record button on the camera before you came in. When I got to set this morning, the crew was watching what happened last night."

Maya clapped her hand over her mouth. "Oh my goodness, you're kidding," she said.

"Don't worry," said Will. "They think we were running lines. For a new ending. And everyone's excited about it."

Maya let Will's words sink in. Back to the tree. The original source of their discord. It was so simple...yet so perfect. She opened her mouth to say something, but Will was moving closer. It felt like the perfect thing to say was nothing at all but to kiss him, with a timer beeping in the background and a whole tray of profiteroles about to overbake but oh well…

Her thoughts scattered the moment Will's lips brushed hers.

"Mmm," he murmured against her lips. "The white chocolate really does add something."

Maya pulled back a bit and grinned. "The unsung hero of the bakery."

Will's eyes twinkling. "What are you doing on Saturday?"

"Nothing. Just working here," she said, still catching her breath.

"Did the kid work out?"

"Working on him. But I think he'll be just fine."

"Good," Will said, his tone soft but serious. "Because I want you beside me on set. Come direct the last scene with me."

Maya's heart soared. "Really?"

"Really," he confirmed, his gaze steady. "In fact, I can't do it without you."

Maya melted into Will's arms again, the sound of the timer singing its concern melting away. She'd bake another batch of profiteroles. They'd figure out their different lives. They'd work as a team to bring the ending to life.

Together, they'd bring that happily-ever-after to life. And it would be spectacular.

Epilogue

Maya almost squealed when they turned the corner onto Main Street and saw the line in front of the Sunset County Theater in the distance. There were at least fifty people waiting in a queue on the sidewalk, all bundled up in the cool evening air, big fluffy snowflakes drifting lazily down from the inky black December sky above.

It wasn't a photo wall lined with paparazzi, and she wasn't wearing Dior, but the sight of her small-town residents coming out to support her film felt better than she imagined any appearance in the society section of the newspaper ever could.

Before exiting the car, Maya pulled the visor mirror down and inspected her lipstick, then adjusted her white wool jacket with the faux fur collar.

"You look stunning," Will said. Maya turned to look at him gazing at her with pure admiration. "Just stunning," he repeated, his brown eyes alight in the dim car. "Diamonds on the soles of her shoes," he sang softly.

The compliment washed over her. She wasn't a Hollywood starlet or a supermodel, but Will somehow made her feel like the most beautiful woman in the world. "More like practical snow-proof boots," Maya grinned. "And you don't look so bad yourself."

In his black leather jacket, dark jeans and a pressed collared shirt, he seemed to get more handsome every time she looked at him.

But more than that, with every day they'd spent together since October, which was any weekend Maya could stay at Flour Child late on Friday to stock up for Saturday and get Lucas to manage the bakery so she could make a quick trip to New York, where Will was deep in preproduction meetings for the *Infinite Realm* series. He'd been on the fence about signing the contract, but Jeff had agreed to finance the Melville projects once they were wrapped. When Will saw the mock-ups for the spacecraft they'd be using for the shoot, the film geek in him had fully taken over, and he couldn't resist jumping on board.

It would be a challenging couple of years ahead, but they were confident they'd make it work.

The attraction and mutual respect was evolving into an incredible relationship, so much so that most of their conversations over the past month revolved around how their future together would look.

Maya had already seen an uptick in book sales, and her movie hadn't even aired yet. She'd just signed another three-book contract with her publisher. The idea of being wherever Will was, writing in the day and spending time together at night and on shoot days, was getting more and more enticing.

The bakery was really the only thing tying her down, but Lucas had recently expressed that the idea of taking a gap year after high school was more and more appealing to him. Maya was planning to float the idea to Cassie of teaching him more about pastry making—he'd all but mastered the breads under her tutelage and had a real knack for it—and having him comanage the bakery for a year. That way, he could take a few online courses to boost his grades and think more deeply about his next steps rather than what he "should do."

The future was so bright and full of possibility that Maya woke up every morning bursting with energy, like she was about to explode into rainbows and sparkles and glitter.

And now, a moment she'd been anticipating for so long.

"Ready to walk the snowy white carpet?" Will asked, a wide grin on his face. He grabbed her hand and pulled it up to his lips, kissing it gently.

"So ready," Maya said. "But this must be old hat for you."

"Honestly," he said, "it really never gets old."

Wearing her dress that was a purposeful balance of nice for photos but also somewhat warm because, dang, it was cold out, Maya exited the car onto Main Street. A light glowed in the window of Flour Child, lighting up the film poster she'd printed to hang in celebration of the release day.

Hand in hand, Maya and Will approached the theater, where a van from the Pinecrest Haven was just pulling in.

"He made it," Maya said, glancing sideways at Will.

He turned to look at her and gave her a tight grin. After selling the house, Will had visited Sunset County three times to see her. Trips to visit Gene, where they purposefully kept the conversation light, had been enjoyable. Gene had settled into his new home and even befriended a woman named Eleanor, who was hard of hearing. She seemed happy to tolerate Gene's rants in exchange for companionship.

The van rolled to a stop, and the driver opened the door. The nurse, who'd been sitting up front, stepped out to assist the residents, helping them one by one onto the freshly shoveled sidewalk.

"There's my real date," Maya said, a playful smile tugging at her lips as she extended her elbow to Gene.

One of the staff members opened the theater door for them, and Maya and Will escorted the nursing home residents inside, guiding them to a special section reserved just for them, ahead of the general public.

Twenty minutes later, Maya sat in the front row, nerves and excitement rushing through her. Despite her many pleas and bribes ranging from cinnamon buns to promises to accompany him to some arthouse film fest that she'd rather gouge out her eyeballs than endure, Will hadn't let her see the earlier cuts. Along with the rest of the Sunset Country residents, this was going to be her first time screening the film.

The owner of the theater took to the mic. "Good evening, ladies and gentlemen," she announced, her voice carrying through the room. "Welcome to the premiere of *Love on the Slopes*!"

The audience erupted into applause, and Will squeezed Maya's hand gently. She looked up at him, and he winked. "Love you," he mouthed, the warmth of his words settling in her chest.

"Before we begin, let's give it up for two very special Sunset County residents, Maya Monroe and Will Hastings!"

The applause was even louder this time, and Maya's

smile stretched so wide she thought it might break her face. She turned to wave at the crowd, the bright stage lights blinding her from making out any faces in the sea of people, but the energy in the room was palpable. She felt the love, the goodwill and the pride swelling inside her. It was surreal.

"Now I'll invite you to sit back and get right into the holiday season! Will and Maya invite you all to mingle in the lobby after the show for shortbread cookies, which, I might add, are from Maya's Flour Child bakery."

"Shortbreads?" Will whispered.

"Too much nervous energy," Maya whispered back. "I might have opened the bakery a little earlier than usual today."

The lights in the theater dimmed, and Maya's heart leaped into her chest the moment the opening crane shot came into focus.

Main Street looked like a holiday dream all decked out in garland and lights...and the snow! The snow was more glorious than she could have ever dreamed of.

And it only got better from there. The acting, the musical cues, the seamless editing and light humor interspersed throughout...and just when Maya thought it couldn't possibly get any better, they hit the bakery scene.

The theater erupted in applause again while Maya was bent over laughing in her chair, tears in her eyes. She had to hand it to herself—her performance was pretty good! It was no surprise a career in acting hadn't panned out for her, but her hair and makeup really did look perfect, and Flour Child glowed with holiday perfection. The magic of it all hit her again, and for a moment, everything felt perfect.

Several times throughout the ninety-minute film, Maya sensed Will looking at her, and every time she turned her head, she found him studying her expression. What she thought of the movie meant something to him, and she was certain she wasn't disappointing him.

When the ending played, and Ben told Sarah that he'd never really believed in weddings until she came along, the theater erupted again in hoots and applause. And then the credits rolled, and Maya sat in admiration watching the names of all the people who'd helped to bring her story to life: Cam, Caroline, Shauna, Stu, Skylar, all the extras and grips and gaffers and script coordinators…and Will.

She followed Will wordlessly out of the theater, thanking everyone who tugged on the sleeve of her dress to say they loved the movie, and emerged into the foyer.

There was not only a bar set up ready to take drink orders, but also Lucas and two of his buddies, dressed in blue jeans and blazers and holding trays of champagne flutes ready to pass around.

"Was this your doing?" Maya said, turning to Will.

Will just smiled and shrugged. "It's your first premiere. Bubbly is a requirement. I got in touch with Lucas to see if he and his friends wanted to make a few bucks."

Lucas's eyes lit up when he saw Maya, and she laughed out loud at the sight of him, all dressed up, mostly.

"Honestly, I normally hate those kinds of movies," Lucas said. "But that was actually all right."

"High praise from you," she said.

He plucked a glass from the tray and handed it to her. "Congrats, Maya. That was pretty cool."

"Thank you," she said. "And are these your friends?"

"This is Dylan," Lucas said. "And Freddie."

"Nice to meet you," said Maya. They both had that look in their eyes, that the second no one was looking, a couple of those flutes were about to go missing and the underagers were going to join in the celebration. She hoped they had fun.

She plucked a flute off the tray for Will, and they stood to the side, watching the residents of Sunset County mingle in the lobby.

"I think that was really sweet, what you did for that kid," said Will. "I know something about feeling a little more than lost in high school."

"But you were a straight-A student," Maya reminded him. "Valedictorian, remember? Top of the class?"

"That came with its own pressures," said Will. "But let's not talk about that. This is your night."

"Our night," Maya corrected and clinked her glass against his. "And the ending," she said, sighing, "really was perfection."

"Agreed," said Will, his voice softening. "You've shown me that a perfect happy ending carries a lot of power."

"I'm glad you finally came around," she whispered, her eyes locking with his.

Before he could respond, Gene approached slowly with the nurse by his side and took Will by the elbow. "You did good, kid," he said. "My mind must really be going because I actually liked that movie."

Maya smiled as she watched Will shake his father's hand. *Not perfect, but better*, she thought. Maybe that was enough.

After the last guest left, Maya and Will got in the car and drove back to her place.

"I really wish you weren't leaving in the morning," she said.

"Me, too," said Will. "But I can't wait to be back for Christmas."

They let themselves in the door, and the sound of Bruce shaking his head and his collar jingling rang from her bedroom. Maya flicked on the flight as Bruce bounded down the hall.

"Come here, baby," she said. "You did such a good job in the movie! Everyone loved you!"

"Speaking of happy endings," Will said as Bruce leaped into her arms.

Maya nestled her face into Bruce's fur, then felt a cold extra piece jiggle on Bruce's collar. She pulled back, her gaze locking onto the gold band dangling from his collar. A diamond glimmered faintly in the dim light of the hallway.

Her breath caught. Was it…

"I knew I wouldn't have to train him to run to you," Will said. "What do you think, Maya? Will you be my happily-ever-after?"

Maya gasped as Will opened the collar, removed the ring and slid it on her finger. "You're definitely a diamonds girl," he said, his grin impossibly warm.

"It's perfect," she whispered and looked up at him, a lump forming in her throat. "You're perfect."

"So that's a yes?" said Will. "'Cause there's more champagne in the fridge and a cake that you didn't even have to bake, and I know you have to get up early, so…"

Maya burst into laughter and fell into Will's arms.

"We're not going to bed tonight," she said, her words wrapped in a playful promise.

"Did you—"

"Lucas is reporting for duty at 5:00 a.m.," Maya said. "He said he was heading home to bed as soon as we left. On a Friday night. Who'd have thought?"

Will kissed the top of her head, then took her hand in his, holding it up to admire the ring that now symbolized their future. He gazed at Maya, and she could tell that in this moment, his own hope and optimism finally mirrored hers. "Who'd have thought, indeed."

* * * * *

Get up to 4 Free Books!

We'll send you 2 free books from each series you try PLUS a free Mystery Gift.

FREE Value Over **$25**

Both the **Harlequin® Special Edition** and **Harlequin® Heartwarming™** series feature compelling novels filled with stories of love and strength where the bonds of friendship, family and community unite.

YES! Please send me 2 FREE novels from the Harlequin Special Edition or Harlequin Heartwarming series and my FREE Gift (gift is worth about $10 retail). After receiving them, if I don't wish to receive any more books, I can return the shipping statement marked "cancel." If I don't cancel, I will receive 6 brand-new Harlequin Special Edition books every month and be billed just $6.39 each in the U.S. or $7.19 each in Canada, or 4 brand-new Harlequin Heartwarming Larger-Print books every month and be billed just $7.19 each in the U.S. or $7.99 each in Canada, a savings of 20% off the cover price. It's quite a bargain! Shipping and handling is just 50¢ per book in the U.S. and $1.25 per book in Canada.* I understand that accepting the 2 free books and gift places me under no obligation to buy anything. I can always return a shipment and cancel at any time by calling the number below. The free books and gift are mine to keep no matter what I decide.

Choose one:
- ☐ **Harlequin Special Edition** (235/335 BPA G36Y)
- ☐ **Harlequin Heartwarming Larger-Print** (161/361 BPA G36Y)
- ☐ **Or Try Both!** (235/335 & 161/361 BPA G36Z)

Name (please print)

Address   Apt. #

City   State/Province   Zip/Postal Code

Email: Please check this box ☐ if you would like to receive newsletters and promotional emails from Harlequin Enterprises ULC and its affiliates. You can unsubscribe anytime.

Mail to the Harlequin Reader Service:
IN U.S.A.: P.O. Box 1341, Buffalo, NY 14240-8531
IN CANADA: P.O. Box 603, Fort Erie, Ontario L2A 5X3

Want to explore our other series or interested in ebooks? Visit www.ReaderService.com or call 1-800-873-8635.

---

*Terms and prices subject to change without notice. Prices do not include sales taxes, which will be charged (if applicable) based on your state or country of residence. Canadian residents will be charged applicable taxes. Offer not valid in Quebec. This offer is limited to one order per household. Books received may not be as shown. Not valid for current subscribers to the Harlequin Special Edition or Harlequin Heartwarming series. All orders subject to approval. Credit or debit balances in a customer's account(s) may be offset by any other outstanding balance owed by or to the customer. Please allow 4 to 6 weeks for delivery. Offer available while quantities last.

Your Privacy—Your information is being collected by Harlequin Enterprises ULC, operating as Harlequin Reader Service. For a complete summary of the information we collect, how we use this information and to whom it is disclosed, please visit our privacy notice located at https://corporate.harlequin.com/privacy-notice. Notice to California Residents – Under California law, you have specific rights to control and access your data. For more information on these rights and how to exercise them, visit https://corporate.harlequin.com/california-privacy. For additional information for residents of other U.S. states that provide their residents with certain rights with respect to personal data, visit https://corporate.harlequin.com/other-state-residents-privacy-rights/.